BRIGHT NOTES

ANIMAL FARM
BY
GEORGE ORWELL

Intelligent Education

INFLUENCE
PUBLISHERS

Nashville, Tennessee

BRIGHT NOTES: Animal Farm
www.BrightNotes.com

No part of this publication may be used or reproduced in any manner whatsoever without written permission, except in the case of brief quotations in critical articles and reviews. For permissions, contact Influence Publishers http://www.influencepublishers.com.

ISBN: 978-1-645421-70-2 (Paperback)
ISBN: 978-1-645421-71-9 (eBook)

Published in accordance with the U.S. Copyright Office Orphan Works and Mass Digitization report of the register of copyrights, June 2015.

Originally published by Monarch Press.
Ralph Ranald; Laurie Rozakis, 1965
2020 Edition published by Influence Publishers.

Interior design by Lapiz Digital Services. Cover Design by Thinkpen Designs.

Printed in the United States of America.

Library of Congress Cataloging-in-Publication Data forthcoming.
Names: Intelligent Education
Title: BRIGHT NOTES: Animal Farm
Subject: STU004000 STUDY AIDS / Book Notes

CONTENTS

GEORGE ORWELL

In 1943, the year of Europe's greatest self-destruction and for Western civilization possibly the most hopeless year of this century, George Orwell published an essay called "Looking Back on the Spanish War." In that essay, there appears a poem dedicated to an anonymous soldier of the war, a war (1936-39) in which Orwell himself served as a volunteer. Orwell had seen the soldier who was the subject of his poem, and whose name he never did learn, in 1936 soon after he had come to Spain to be a soldier in the revolutionary militia.

The poem is not a great one; Orwell was not primarily a poet. But the last **stanza** is of some significance for a consideration of the man George Orwell as well as his work. Orwell addresses this unknown soldier, who stands for all ordinary soldiers who fought in this destructive Civil War in Spain:

But the thing that I saw in your face No power can disinherit: No bomb that ever burst, Shatters the crystal spirit.

"No bomb that ever burst, shatters the crystal spirit." The line is typical of Orwell. It could stand as an epigraph or slogan, though he himself was skeptical of slogans, for George Orwell's own life and what he stood for, or thought he stood for: the dignity of man, the inviolability of the human spirit, and each man's right to spiritual privacy. Man has, in the language of the American Declaration of Independence, "certain inalienable rights," and it is the inalienability of these rights which Orwell affirmed in all his works, whether they are novels, as is *1984*, or political satires, such as *Animal Farm*, or individual essays on literary, political, and social matters, or books such as *Burmese Days* or *Homage to Catalonia*, which might best be called "political autobiographies." Consequently, it is something of a paradox that Orwell's deservedly great reputation today rests primarily on *1984*, a work which seems to contain the deepest pessimism about man's nature. But the two views of Orwell, as a pessimist about man's capacity for the total enslavement of his fellows, and as an optimist and affirmer of the human spirit, can be reconciled by study of his biography and of the body of his writings, especially as they bear on that biography.

1984 is a dark work, at least on the surface, and there seems little of affirmation about it. It has given words and phrases to the English language: Thoughtcrime, Newspeak, Big Brother, the Two Minutes' Hate, the Proles, the Thought Police. But these, all of which are concepts characterizing the nightmare world of *1984*, require further explanation than that provided in the novel and that explanation may be found in large measure in the biography of George Orwell. While works such as *1984* and *Down and Out in Paris and London* may stand alone and be read without reference to biographical material, a consideration of that material casts additional light on their meaning. It is to that biography that we now turn.

Orwell was born Eric Hugh Blair in 1903 in Motihari, Bengal, an area in eastern India only about three hundred miles from Burma, where Orwell was to serve twenty years later as a British civil servant. He was the only son of a subordinate British civil servant; his father, serving in the British Raj (government) of India, worked in the Customs and Excise department the government. Apparently Orwell's father was reserved and distant with his children. Orwell had a sister about five years old than he, and another five years younger, but he was never very close to his sisters either. Indeed, by his own account his attitude toward his immediate family was largely negative (except for his relationship with his mother). This attitude is revealed in what Orwell said about his early childhood in his famous essay "Such, Such Were the Joys ..." which deals with his unhappy career at an English preparatory school. As a salaried official without an independent income, Orwell's father does not seem to have been well off financially. This poverty was to haunt our novelist, causing him to dwell almost obsessively on matters of social class and social distinction. Indeed, Orwell was on one occasion to describe the social class into which he was born as "lower upper-middle," perhaps with a touch of **irony** at such attempts at precise classification.

In 1911, at a very early age, Orwell was sent back to England to begin his education. These were the last quiet years of the pre-World War I era, when the imperial power of England was unquestioned and when it was necessary to have a constant supply of young men who, learning the art and science of ruling in England, would come out to India, Burma, and other far reaches of the British Empire to staff the government offices. And such a career - his father's - seems at this point to have been Orwell's destiny. Thus, the lengthy enforced separation from his family - there was certainly not enough money for the boy to make visits back to India - followed a quite usual pattern among the English upper and middle classes. The educational system which was based on a rather rigid class structure had narrow but clearly defined goals based on a philosophy of education which had been developing in England at least since the sixteenth century. This system was to have a profound effect on George Orwell, much of whose writing was to become either a commentary on or a criticism of it.

The preparatory school he attended beginning at age eight was located on the southern coast of England; it is the school to which he referred, though not by its actual name, in the essay "Such, Such Were the Joys ..." This essay is a biting, indeed a bitter attack on the kind of education which was respected among certain social classes in Great Britain; and although Orwell disguised the name of the school by calling it "Crossgates" the essay has still never been legally published in England because of the possibility of a libel suit involving the good name of the school. Orwell was to be a boarding student at the school for five years, from 1911 through 1916.

Orwell's parents seem to have been less well-to-do than the parents of most of the other students at "Crossgates." Orwell relates in his essay that by indirect means he gradually came to realize that Mr. and Mrs. Simpson, the Headmaster and Headmistress of the school (nicknamed by the boys respectively Sim and Bingo) had taken on young George, or Eric, as he was then called, as a sort of investment, at reduced tuition and boarding fees. However, as he saw the case, they did this not out of concern for his welfare, but rather because they thought he was bright and expected that with proper instruction he would win valuable scholarships to some of the great public schools, such as Eton, Winchester, or Wellington. This achievement would in turn help to add luster to the school's name and, as it was a private institution run in some measure for profit, attract more and wealthier students to it. The boy did not disappoint them in this respect, because he won scholarships both to Eton, which he ultimately attended and which is one of the most famous as well as one of the oldest public schools in England, and to Wellington.

But there were a number of things about the preparatory school which he detested, and which, from his own account, were to scar him psychologically. Thus, even the title of his essay is a bitterly ironic one. In his Songs of Innocence, the eighteenth-century poet William Blake has a poem called "The Ecchoing Green," the middle **stanza** of which paints a picture of the idealized innocence and joyfulness of childhood:

Old John, with white hair, Does laugh away care, Sitting under the oak, Among the old folk. They laugh at our play, And soon they all say: "Such, such were the joys When we all, girls and boys, In our youth time were seen On the Ecchoing Green."

But for the young Eric Blair, there were to be no idyllic times at Crossgates. He was rudely awakened by the stern regimen of the school. Beatings were commonplace. He recounts in the essay that soon after he arrived, at age eight, he was beaten by the Headmaster, Sim, for wetting his bed. He initially made light of the beating, though it was with a bone-handled riding crop; however, Sim overheard him tell his fellow students outside the room that "It didn't hurt," and he was immediately beaten again. This time the Headmaster used such force that he broke the handle of the riding crop while beating him to the point where he collapsed "into a chair, weakly snivelling."

This beating marked the start of an educational process which was to instill in the young Eric Blair an awful conviction of worthlessness, guilt, and weakness, which by his own account, he was not able to overcome for years. "This was," he wrote in "Such, Such Were the Joys ...," "the great abiding lesson of my boyhood: that I was in a world where it was not possible for me to be good ... it brought home to me for the first time the harshness of the environment into which I had been flung." He did not add, though he might have, that the real or fancied maltreatment at Crossgates was not only to scar him psychologically, but to develop in him certain characteristic interests, to intensify his preoccupation with certain themes, such as the effect of prolonged punishment on the human spirit, the relative importance of heredity and environment, the possibility of brainwashing (especially important in *1984)*, and the oppression, as he saw it, so often visited on the defenseless, whether they were the poor of India or Burma, or the unassertive English boarding-school student such as he fancied himself to be at this time. At Crossgates, the boy was beaten for being a chronic bed-wetter - something which he literally could not help - and underwent the usual "fagging" [hazing] at the hands of the older boys. What he especially resented was the favoritism which he believed he saw in the treatment meted out by the Headmaster: the boys whose parents were wealthy and titled were treated with much more consideration than were the poorer boys who were attending the school at reduced tuition rates.

The formal curriculum had the classical bias usual at such a school; the students started Latin at age eight, Greek at age ten. But much of the learning in the classical languages was to Eric Blair the dullest kind of rote learning. He was, as a scholarship student, being prepared to take a competitive examination at age twelve or thirteen - an examination which would determine his entire future. For if he was successful in it, he would win a scholarship to a public school; if he failed, he would undoubtedly become, as the Headmaster frequently told him, "a little office boy at forty pounds a year." The studies emphasized anything which might contribute to his passing the examination, but he felt that while the system may have been efficient in that it achieved its objective, it could not truly be called education.

Though Bingo and Sim frequently reminded him of how much they had done for him, a scholarship boy who was "living on their bounty," he was not grateful. Instead, he said in "Such, Such Were the Joys..." "I hated both of them. I could not control my subjective feelings, and I could not control them from myself." This point in Orwell's biography may be important for the light it casts on the ambivalent way in which Winston Smith, the oppressed little man representative of much in his society in *1984*, regards Big Brother, For the young Eric Blair, the authorities of his preparatory school, especially Sim and Bingo, stood in the same relationship to him as did Big Brother to Winston Smith; indeed the latter situation may well have been suggested by the former. The lack of privacy in the living quarters of the school, the oppression with the encouragement of Sim and Bingo, of the weaker boys by the stronger, the spying, especially in search of heterodox behavior or sexual misdemeanors among the boys, the "squalor and neglect... the W. C. [water closet, or lavatory] and dirty-handkerchief side of life," as Orwell called it-all these were to appear in his writing, though changed and magnified. The worst thing about Crossgates, then, in Orwell's view was that it violated his integrity, and attempted to deny to him the sole possession of that corner of his mind or consciousness which was, or should have been, forever and inalienably his. This **theme**, too, of the ultimate blasphemy of the violation of sovereign personality, reappears in *1984*.

In fairness to the proprietors of Crossgates, it must be said that Orwell's view of the school and the influence it was to have on his life and thought was highly subjective (as he himself stated in his essay about this period of his life.) Christopher Hollis, a friend and contemporary of George Orwell at Eton and the author of a biographical-critical study of him (see Bibliography) refers to the Crossgates **episode** in more balanced terms, as though the school was not objectively quite as bad as Orwell painted it - though some of the abuses which Orwell mentioned no doubt did in fact exist. But the important point is not the objective reality of the school, but the effect which it had on Orwell during a key phase in his development. He had a sense of inferiority and failure which haunted him. In a world made for the strong, he was convinced that he was doomed not to succeed, because in any case, in the terms of the rigid social code drummed into him at Crossgates, "success was measured not by what you did but by what you were." Even after he had won his two excellent scholarships, to Eton and to Wellington, he felt that Sim and Bingo and the school rejected him. He was not in good health, having defective bronchial tubes and a minor lesion on one lung which, it may be, helped to occasion his untimely death at age forty-seven. But beyond any physical deficiencies, real or imagined, was the awful sense of failure and of the bonds of class and birth. "In a world where the prime necessities were money, titled relatives, athleticism, tailor-made clothes, neatly brushed hair, a charming smile, I was no good." Such were his words about himself at the time he left Crossgates forever.

By his proficiency at Crossgates in the study of Latin and Greek, under the urgings (and beatings) of Sim and Bingo, Orwell won a scholarship which would maintain him at Eton for a complete education, provided his scholastic performance was satisfactory. Thus, in 1917, when Orwell was fourteen years old, he matriculated at Eton. In the public schools the students were given much more freedom to manage their own affairs that was the case at the preparatory schools, and as Orwell himself said in "Such, Such Were the Joys ...," he became an idler where his studies were concerned. After the years of cramming in Latin and Greek, he did only enough at Eton to maintain a class standing that would permit him to retain his scholarship, and no more. But he read widely, and even at this point in his life he impressed those around him as being an intellectual. To Cyril Connolly (see Bibliography) one of his acquaintances at Eton, he proved by the force of his example "that there existed an alternative to character, Intelligence." His reading included Shaw, Samuel Butler, and others who might be described as the great questioners of Victorian life, and whose practice reinforced Orwell's own tendency to ask embarrassing questions about society.

While Orwell said that he was not well liked by the other boys at Eton, in part because of his poverty, this does not seem to be true. Christopher Hollis, two years ahead of him at Eton and therefore roughly his contemporary in the school, says that Orwell was regarded as something of a leader of the other boys, and also that in an environment in which beatings were a part of the system, he was in fact beaten rather less than the others. But Orwell's final judgment on Eton, published in an article in the Observer, "For Ever Eton," on August 1, 1948, described the school as offering "a tolerant and civilized atmosphere which gives each boy a fair chance of developing his individuality."

Orwell graduated from Eton at age eighteen, and rather unexpectedly, was to spend the next five years (1922-27) in Burma as an officer of the Indian Imperial Police. For a young man graduating from a public school like Eton, the normal next step would have been entrance to Oxford or Cambridge for three years of further study and a University degree. And apparently

Orwell could have had this, for Eton provided scholarships for some of its students who might not otherwise have had the opportunity to attend a University. Though the circumstances are somewhat obscure, Orwell, according to Christopher Hollis, was persuaded by one of his teachers at Eton that he ought to bypass the University route. "You've had enough of education. Take a job abroad and see something of the world," his teacher allegedly told him, and though Orwell was rather to regret this decision later, he entered the service of the British Government as a civil servant in Burma.

He apparently was a good officer, for he did have the habit of command. But he became increasingly disillusioned with his job, and ceased to believe in the beneficial effects of imperialism, even British imperialism. He felt that all Europeans, as he said in his essay "Marrakech," are essentially fooling the peoples under colonial domination, and he developed, during his five years in the British service, a tremendous amount of guilt at his supposedly privileged position. This guilt feeling simply reinforced the feeling of general "worthlessness" which had been built up during his preparatory school years. His experience in Burma is perhaps best illustrated in the famous essay "Shooting an Elephant," written a number of years after the fact, in which his performance of his duty as a police officer in Moulmein, Lower Burma, becomes the occasion for a graphic comment on what he saw as the essential self-imprisonment of all who served the cause of the British Government in its imperial domains.

Feeling stifled, therefore, by his job Orwell came home on leave in 1927 and never returned to Burma, instead resigning from the service. The Burmese experience was very valuable to him is his formation as an artist and a thinker, but torture to him as a man because of his sensitivity to what he thought of as the shortcomings of imperialism. Out of his Burmese experience was to come his first novel, *Burmese Days,* published in 1934, seven years after his return from Burma. As is the case in every Orwell novel, there is one character in *Burmese Days* who has many of the qualities of Orwell himself, and with whom Orwell consciously or unconsciously identified. That character is named Flory-also a civil servant in the British Raj in Burma who deteriorates under the influence of the system. But Orwell himself, fearing that the system would ruin him both ethically and emotionally if he remained a part of it, left the service, while Flory stayed in it until it indirectly at least brought about his death.

From 1927 until 1933 Orwell led what must have been an unprecedented life for a young man of his ability and education. Explanations of his motivation for leading this life are still vague; perhaps the truth will never be known. But out of these years of great poverty and deprivation came, in 1933, his first book, *Down and Out in Paris and London,* a most graphic and subjective study of poverty and its effect upon the human spirit, and certainly one of the most truthful books on the subject that has ever been written.

Orwell at this time changed his name from Eric Blair. "George" is a traditional English name, the patron Saint of England being St. George, who is known for fighting with dragons, as Orwell metaphorically fought with himself and the world. "Orwell" is the name of a small river in Suffolk, by which he once lived; the symbolism of this name may involve simply his returning to the land, the earth, out of the rarefied background of an Etonian education. But his reasons are really obscure. It appears that he had such a strong feeling of guilt over the class privilege from which he had benefited, first at Eton and then in Burma, that he rejected this privilege and turned his back on his social class by changing his name and living in poverty for nearly six years. The concern with the sheer physical side of poverty and deprivation which we find in *1984* stems from this period in Orwell's life.

After his return from the lower depths of poverty in 1933, a year which, significantly, coincided with the rise to power of Hitler in Germany, Orwell averaged about a book a year until World War II and his declining health made this rate of literary production impossible. Poverty, whether lower-class or, something which he personally regarded as worse, lower middle-class, was his subject in his next two novels, *A Clergyman's Daughter* (1935), and *Keep the Aspidistra Flying* (1936).

The first is a book about the impoverishment, physical and spiritual, of moneyless middle-class genteel life in an English vicarage and in a dreadful and cheap girls' private school. The second is an even more powerful work about a conflict between Bohemianism and normal middle-class respectability which at least affirms the continuance of life; the hero, Gordon Comstock, strongly resembles Orwell himself. Both novels cast some light on Orwell's preoccupations in his masterpiece, *1984*, with those pressures which erode the human spirit. Two of the worst of these are poverty and deprivation, tools which the Party in *1984* uses because it desires the degradation of man.

By 1936, he was earning enough from writing - no small trick in an England still undergoing the depression - to live in the country away from London. In 1936 he began a survey of unemployment in England and its effects. This resulted in 1937 in *The Road to Wigan Pier*, which the Left Book Club, which commissioned it, was to print while at the same time disclaiming responsibility for the views Orwell expressed in it. In this book he spoke of socialism as a possible remedy for the conditions which he so excellently described out of firsthand knowledge and emotional understanding.

He married Eileen O'Shaughnessy in 1936, and the marriage seems to have been a happy one, even an ideal relationship. Leaving the manuscript of *The Road to Wigan Pier* with those who had commissioned it, before they could argue with him over its content, Orwell and his wife went to Spain, where the Spanish Civil War had broken out in that year. Orwell wished to study the Civil War and had received a publisher's advance to write a book about it. Quite characteristically, he decided that the best way to study the war was to fight in it. He became a member of the P. O. U. M. (Partido Obrero de Unificacion Marxista, translated as Workers' Party of Marxist Unification). This was a radical Socialist-Trotskyite militia force which was opposed to the Communist-Stalinists of the International Brigades. As it turned out, the two factions ended up fighting each other as bitterly as they were to fight the Fascist forces of General Francisco Franco. The P. O. U. M. was ruthlessly suppressed by Stalin's agents and their collaborators, and many Spanish members who had joined the P. O. U. M. wishing only to fight those who had rebelled against the Republican Government of Spain were arrested and executed. Orwell was badly wounded in the throat in fighting on the front lines, and then was under such suspicion as a member of the P. O. U. M. that he and his wife were lucky to escape from Spain with their lives. It is probable that his being a British subject helped him to escape, but others among his friends were not so lucky, and were killed or died in prison. This experience acquainted him at firsthand with the nature of totalitarianism, for Spain, from 1936 to 1939, may be described, though the terms are over-simplified, as a battleground between the two chief forms of totalitarian regime of our century, fascism and communism. Out of this period came Orwell's book about his experience in Spain, *Homage to Catalonia* (1938). Orwell regarded the actions of the Communists in Spain as a betrayal of the popular revolution which might otherwise have given the working classes real freedom and status. This idea is to spill over into the presentation of the Party in *1984* and the divergence between its theory and its practice.

Nineteen Hundred and Thirty Nine saw the publication of *Coming Up for Air,* a combination of nostalgia for pre-World War I times and conservative England, and apprehension at the appearance of "the streamlined men from Eastern Europe, who thought in slogans and spoke in bullets." After 1939, with the outbreak of World War II, Orwell devoted himself to writing on behalf of the war effort and to service as a sergeant in the Home Guard in England (he was rejected for military service because of his impaired health). He broadcast and wrote for the B. B. C., and also wrote many essays, containing qualified but sincere praise of English institutions and ways when compared with the ways of the totalitarian regimes of Hitler, Mussolini, and Stalin. As a result of his Spanish experience, Orwell was less deceived than most about Stalin's objectives in allowing Russia's entry into the war in 1941. And even in the fever of war hysteria, when England was fighting for its very existence, Orwell spoke out for reason and for the facing of cold facts, whether about the Germans or about those who were less frank in their devotion to dictatorial forms of government. All totalitarianism was wrong, in Orwell's view, as it involved a denial of the basic dignity of man. Thus *The Lion and the Unicorn*, published in 1941, was a pamphlet containing three essays: "Shopkeepers at War," "The English Revolution," and "England, Your England." The last of these is the most famous, but all three describe what Orwell thinks of the English people. On a comparative basis, he says, they at least are more devoted than most to the principles of decency and human freedom which make life worth living.

Animal Farm, which with *1984* would make Orwell world famous, was written between November, 1943, and February, 1944. For some time Orwell was unable to find a publisher for it. This was due in part to the wartime condition of paper scarcity, but also to the fact that Russia was an ally and it was perceived that *Animal Farm* was a **satire** on the rise of totalitarian government in Russia under Lenin, Trotsky, and Stalin. It is political satire-especially reminiscent of Book IV of *Gulliver's Travels*-perhaps the best English satire on communism. Its genesis was really in Orwell's experience in Spain, as has been pointed out, and when *Animal Farm* finally appeared in August, 1945, it was at that point where the Western Allies were becoming disenchanted with the Stalin regime and the possibilities of cooperating with it in the construction of a viable postwar order. Thus, the hour and the book were exactly matched, and the inevitable result was that Orwell's book, being widely translated, became world famous.

In this year, 1945, Orwell's wife died as the result of a minor operation. He attributed her death to lowered physical resistance due to the war; both she and Orwell had consistently given up a part of their wartime food rations to feed children, and consequently had impaired their health. But this was in keeping with their character; both have been described by friends as having something of the saintly ascetic in their makeups.

1984 came out of the chaotic postwar period, 1945-49, and was written in the state of depression and pessimism occasioned by the unexpected death of Orwell's wife and by his own poor health. In this period he learned that he was suffering from tuberculosis, and that he would have to rest if his life were to be saved. Instead, out of a sense of duty and an overwhelming urge to express what he had learned of totalitarianism, he wrote *1984.* Off the coast of western Scotland, about a hundred miles west of Glasgow, there is an island off the beaten track: the island of Jura. There, in 1947, Orwell went with the infant son whom he and his wife had adopted, taking along his sister to act as the nurse, and there he worked to finish *1984.* In January, 1949, *1984* was finished, and his friend Richard Rees accompanied him from Jura to a sanitarium in Gloucestershire.

Orwell's health was shattered. He had a few months of happiness in 1949 when in the early summer he married Sonia Brownell, who assisted him in taking care of his adopted son. On January 21, 1950, as he was about to leave for a sanitarium in Switzerland, he had a tubercular hemmorhage and died. While it is clear that the condition of his health in his last years had something to do with the thoughts he expressed in *1984,* and the personal tragedies he underwent also contributed to this end, it must be remembered that essentially all of his life and work was a preparation for writing *1984;* this is one of the reasons for studying his biography and his other novels and essays carefully quite apart from their intrinsic interest. He was writing in *1984* about what he had once called "the central question ... how to prevent power from being abused." *Animal Farm* was a study and a history of this subject from a different point of view and in a different literary **genre** - the beast fable rather than (as in *1984)* the anti-Utopia. But his abiding preoccupation was with the reconcilement of human liberty and the affirmation of the human spirit with the exercise of power which must of necessity exist if society is to exist. Behind this preoccupation was his belief in the human race and in the necessity of its survival in freedom.

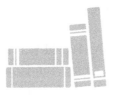

ANIMAL FARM

Before undertaking the detailed analysis of the **satire** of *Animal Farm* it is necessary for the reader to consider the structure of the work and the levels of meaning on which it operates. While the discussion of levels of meaning on which a work may be read can be carried far beyond what is reasonable, it must here be accepted almost as an axiom in geometry that Orwell did not write *Animal Farm* simply as an animal story or fable suitable for the entertainment of children, any more than did Jonathan Swift, one of Orwell's literary masters, wrote *Gulliver's Travels* as children's' entertainment, though both masterpieces can serve very well for this purpose among others. (Serious students of literature may wish to read some of the cleverly satiric essays in Frederick C. Crews, The Pooh Perplex, New York: E. P. Dutton and Co., Inc., 1963, on this point.)

Animal Farm may be read on at least four levels: (1) The entertaining animal story, fable, or (as Orwell himself called it) fairy story. (2) A history of the development of Communist theory under Lenin and Stalin. (3) A history of Russia including its foreign relations from the October Revolution (1917) to the uneasy relationship between Russia and the Western democracies as the Second World War drew to its close (1944-45). (4) At the deepest, most fundamental level, an account of the way revolutions are made and subsequently corrupted, of the way men form political societies and exercise power in those societies, and finally, an illustration of the famous dictum on the nineteenth-century British historian, Lord Acton: "Power corrupts, and absolute power corrupts absolutely." This fourth level has little to do directly with the history or the evolution of communism, as it is rather directed towards Orwell's view of human nature in general.

Having identified these levels, one should not take them too seriously. The balance of humor and serious **satire** in *Animal Farm* is a delicate one, easily destroyed by too close and overly serious analysis. Animal figures have been used for many centuries, whether by primitive tellers of tales and legends whose names are unknown and whose work has come down to us, if at all, by distorted oral tradition, or by highly conscious and highly sophisticated artists, among whom may be classed Swift and Orwell. And they have been used to embody truth about human beings, by attributing to the animals various human qualities, sometimes in exaggerated measure. Probably one of the justifications for the use of fabulous animal figures to convey human truth lies in human psychology-in the perception of sameness in difference which the reader of an animal story or fable obtains when he is presented with animals who manifest, usually in exaggerated form, human characteristics, and when he, the reader, is thus forced to suspend his disbelief and to enter into the spirit of the animal fable, which he will in proportion as the fable embodies evident truth.

Aesop, a Greek slave thought to have lived about 600 B.C., is the presumed author of the most famous animal fables of all time, but was by no means the last great master of this form.

Chaucer's The Nun's Priest's Tale, of the Cock and the Hen, Chaunticleer and Pertelote, is such a beast-fable used to point a human moral. Indeed, medieval literature is full of animal fables and animals used as human symbols. What is perhaps the greatest work of Western literature between the beginning of the Christian era and the time of Shakespeare, the Divine Comedy of Dante, includes animal symbolism in its opening canto among other places, as the **protagonist** of the Comedy, at the beginning of his journey through the Inferno, Purgatory, and Paradise, encounters a leopard, a lion, and a wolf. And these symbols in turn seem to come from the Bible, where of course many such animal symbols are to be found; these are traceable to the Old Testament, to Jeremiah V, 6. This point - that Orwell was writing in *Animal Farm* within a definite and long-standing tradition-needs further elaboration, but it is sufficient for the moment to mention it in order to place *Animal Farm* within the tradition.

The term "fable" has also as one of its definitions "a story which was once believed but which has since turned out to be untrue." *Animal Farm* is thus a fable of Communist revolutionary ideology; part of its structure involves a movement by certain of the animals on the farm away from that which was believed to be objectively true (Marxist ideology, on which the Russian Revolution was presumably based), toward the weakening and ultimate death of belief in such ideology, and finally its replacement by a sham used to keep the less intelligent members of the community from finding out the truth. This theme-one of Orwell's master themes, for which he seemed to have a special affinity and by which he was fascinated-appears in intensified form in *1984* and we shall take up its appearance there separately. Orwell, then, was writing a fable about the weakening and the corruption of a belief which, in his view, may not have been intrinsically either good or evil, but which was made evil by the inevitable corruption attendant upon the exercise of power by fallible men.

But what evidence is there anywhere in *Animal Farm* that the interpretation of this charming book as a political fable or allegory has any validity? Orwell himself nowhere uses the words Communism, Russia, Germany, Marx, Stalin, Lenin, Trotsky in the book; why, then, are his readers so eager to draw political meanings out of the story? Perhaps *Animal Farm* is exactly as it appears on the surface: entertainment for children through the humorous presentation of animals who behave however imperfectly, as humans.

This interpretation of *Animal Farm* as entertainment only must be rejected on the basis of a number of kinds of evidence. Probably most important is the totality of Orwell's life and work, which has been outlined in the Introduction to the present study in a fair amount of detail. His life was a long process of education, beginning at "Crossgates" and Eton, with post graduate work in poverty, imperialist oppression as he saw it, and the culmination of his education in totalitarianism in Spain during 1936-38, with its attendant disillusion with Stalinist terrorism. Orwell was that curious, rare breed of man of letters who was determined to live and to experience those things about which he wrote, whether it was poverty, heavy manual labor in the coal mines, Communism, or Fascism. This process of education resulted in his two masterpieces, *Animal Farm* and *1984*, for his life was a preparation for a blast against totalitarianism and against human greed and folly.

But there is more specific evidence than simply a general consideration of Orwell's biography. In 1947, just as *Animal Farm* had made him famous, Orwell published an essay entitled "Why I Write," reprinted in *A Collection of Essays* (see Bibliography below). In the essay there are two key passages which provide definitive evidence as to Orwell's intention in writing *Animal Farm.* "Every line of serious work that I have written since 1936," Orwell wrote, "has been written, directly or indirectly, against totalitarianism and for democratic socialism, as I understand it. It seems to me nonsense, in a period like our own, to think that one can avoid writing of such subjects. Everyone writes of them in one guise or another. It is simply a question of which side one takes and what approach one follows."

The second passage is even more brief and to the point: "*Animal Farm* was the first book in which I tried, with full consciousness of what I was doing, to fuse political purpose and artistic purpose into one whole ... Looking back through my work, I see that it is invariably where I lacked a political purpose that I wrote lifeless books and was betrayed into purple passages, sentences without meaning, decorative adjectives, and humbug generally." Judging from this statement, the meaning of *Animal Farm* lies in politics and, while most readers who are even remotely acquainted with political history since the First World War would recognize a number of parallels with the events in *Animal Farm,* the evidence we have of Orwell's political intent is stronger than simple likeness of event. We have his purpose stated in his own words, and these words should be accepted at their face value.

Orwell was writing about a political system which had begun full of promise and which had deteriorated into tyranny. One of his purposes in using the figures of beasts to portray the actions of men, though not his only purpose, was to imply that men in their political communities were often no better than beasts, though more is expected of man because of his possession of the faculty of Reason. In the very last line of *Animal Farm,* when the animals, having taken possession of the Farm are now-some of them-walking upright like men, and in other ways imitating the ways of men, Orwell comments dryly: "it was impossible to say which was which." And this is phrased in a way not complimentary to the human race.

The difference between the **satire** of Orwell and that of Jonathan Swift is, for one thing, that Orwell had a much lighter touch. It is to be remembered that **satire** may be defined as a literary manner or **genre** which blends a critical attitude with humor and wit to the end that human institutions may be improved.

Satire tends toward political and social activism in many cases, but if it becomes too dark and draws on overly grim picture of human nature it becomes more vituperation than true corrective **satire**. Some have said that parts of *Gulliver's Travels* manifest too deep a despair over human corruption, and that Swift went too far in symbolizing the moral corruption of mankind by the physical nastiness which appears at a number of points in that great work. Others have said that Swift was only telling the truth and nothing but the truth, and that the contrast of the rational horses, or Houyhnhnms, with the subhuman, or all too human, Yahoos, is no exaggeration.

However, while Swift and Orwell both attacked vices in mankind, through the satiric use of animal characters to represent aspects of human society, a comparative reading of *Animal Farm* and of the Fourth Book of *Gulliver's Travels,* which is the book most resembling *Animal Farm,* generally reveals at least slightly less pessimism on Orwell's part than on Swift's. Man's follies and his almost limitless capacity for being duped and tricked are both funny and tragic to Orwell, but in *Animal Farm* he keeps the humor and the tragedy in nice balance.

The structure of *Animal Farm* may be described as "fabulous history." Proper perspective is attained by representing various historical characters and events on the scale of the farmyard; this is the literary device of "scaling down" for satiric effect, just as if one were looking at the events through the small end of a telescope. The dramatic satirist Bertolt Brecht used a similar device in his play about the rise of Hitler, Arturo Ui, in which Hitler was portrayed as a Chicago gang leader, and the rise of the Nazi Party in Germany as the rise of one gang led by Arturo over rival gangs and over the forces of civic reform. Swift himself used this device, when in *Gulliver's Travels* he really viewed man in the four books of that work from four different perspectives: man as dwarf, as giant, as scatterbrained "projector" (experimenter and disturber of the peace), and finally, in his most depressing manifestation, man as animal and animal as man. And this last is Orwell's device, but we must, as we consider the **satire** of *Animal Farm* and comment on the work in detail, resist the tendency to be overly serious; at the risk of repeating this point, it must be said that while Orwell's purpose was serious, as he himself has told us, his method involved comedy and the light touch with the satiric rapier rather than with the battle-axe Swift sometimes used.

Note

The book is divided into ten chapters, and it seems most convenient to analyze each separately first before proceeding to general critical commentary and the opinions of some of those who expressed their views on the book, with particular attention to what was said about it when it first appeared in 1945.

ANIMAL FARM

CHAPTER ONE

....

In the first chapter, we are introduced to a deteriorating situation on Manor Farm, which in Orwell's political allegory represents Imperial Russia prior to 1917. Mr. Jones (the Tsar, perhaps more specifically Nicholas II, the last Tsar of Russia who was executed by the Russian revolutionaries in 1918) has lost control of the Farm. One night, so drunk that he cannot even remember to shut and lock the animals into their barn and cages, he falls asleep. As Jones is out of the way for the night, the animals of the Farm come to a secret meeting, called by old Major, a majestic-looking pig, who wishes to communicate a strange dream to the other animals in the big barn. At the meeting, Major (probably signifying both Marx and Lenin) gives a spellbinding oration about the oppressed condition of the animals, and introduces them to a new and stirring revolutionary song, Beasts of England (which represents the Communist Internationale). The animals are so delighted with the song that they make a tremendous uproar as they sing it, whereupon Jones is awakened from his drunken sleep and scatters the animals by firing a shotgun into the night; he thinks that a fox is in the yard, but does not suspect that a revolt of the beasts is being plotted.

Comment

Old Major, on the level of sheer history, is probably a combination of Karl Marx and V. I. Lenin. (Vladimir, Ilyich Ulyanov. All of the "big three" founders of Soviet Communism, Lenin, Trotsky, and Stalin, are known by names which they adopted, and here we will give their real names as well as the names by which they have become known to history.) Marx (1818-1883) was of course the prime theoretician of Communism, and it was he who, in the terms of the allegory of *Animal Farm,* dreamed a "strange dream" which he wished to communicate to the others. The dream, of course, is that of the proletarian revolution. Incidentally, the student is referred to an easily available paperback, *Essential Works of Marxism,* edited by Arthur P. Mendel (Library of Basic Ideas: Bantam Books, SC 125, 1961), and to the coming revision of the Monarch Press Study Guide, *An Outline and Criticism of Communist Theory from Marx to Mao*, for a very brief and elementary outline history of the Communist movement beginning with Marx. For while *Animal Farm* may be appreciated by one who knows nothing of this ideological history-indeed, such universality of statement and of appeal is one of Orwell's strengths in *Animal Farm,* as elsewhere in his works-it is hard to see how a reader completely uninformed about this aspect of recent European and world history could fully appreciate *Animal Farm.* This is a reversed statement; making a horrible pun, we may say that it puts the cart before the horse as far as the interpretation and enjoyment of *Animal Farm* are concerned. For *Animal Farm* was written for people who know something of history, and Orwell meant it to be read by them, even if the history came right out of the newspapers and was not subject to the critical and evaluative processes of professional historical scholarship.

The "dream" of Marx, a new religion though a secularized and materialistic one, is stated most succinctly in *The Communist Manifesto* (1848), written in collaboration with Friedrich Engels, and the very first line of this document is this: "The history of all hitherto existing society is the history of class struggles." And this is the thesis of Major's impassioned speech late at night in the barn of Mr. Jones's farm as he exhorts the animals to throw off the chains which bind them. "Man is the only real enemy we have," Major tells his listeners.

But Major is not only the theoretician, he is the moving force of the Revolution on the farm. One must not expect Orwell to have created exact historical characters; to look for exact parallels with history would be to misread *Animal Farm* and to take it too seriously in the wrong way. The same observation applies to the incidents as well as the characters of the story. Major is thus not only Marx, he is also Lenin, who sees the Revolution into being but rules Russia after the Revolution less than seven years, dying prematurely at age fifty-three and leaving to others the task of completing the work of the revolutionary government.

The speech of Major is stirring and provocative to the other animals, most of whom are not nearly as bright as Major. The prize Middle White boar uses exactly the arguments which would appeal to his audience: the soil of England is fertile, there should be enough for everyone, but in all England not a single animal is free, and everywhere Man robs the animals of their just compensation for labor. All this is accepted uncritically. Major had said that he would relate a wonderful dream that he had experienced - but once he has an audience, he stirs it with a rousing speech first and delays the retelling of the dream until the end, for good reason.

What is present in Major's speech is a **burlesque** version of the Marxist theories of class struggle, the labor theory of value, and surplus value, as well as the idea that the animals, who alone are productive (as are the workers, peasants, and intellectuals in Marxist theory), should regard Man, "the only creature that consumes without producing" (the class of the bourgeoisie and the capitalists according to Marx and Lenin), as their enemy and should, in keeping with their duty of enmity toward Man, revolt against his domination.

Of course, this is a fantasy; most of the audience are much too ignorant to see that Major is cleverly playing on them. But Orwell, in a master stroke of **satire**, implies that Major, at least, is probably sincere. He utters a number of Commandments in his speech, as though he were a primal lawgiver; these will be embodied later into a sort of law for *Animal Farm* once the animals have triumphed, and will also be rewritten as, Orwell implied, all principles of all revolutions undergo such changes, for the worse, once the revolutionary spirit is corrupted by knavish leaders who seek only their own ends. "Even when you have conquered Man," says Major, "do not adopt his vices." In his simplistic view of the world, animals must consider themselves entirely good and Man as entirely evil. "All animals are equal" - this is the final message of Major, after he brings the animals to a vote on whether the rats should be considered comrades also, and the vote is in the affirmative.

Finally, Major leads the animals in singing Beasts of England, which as has been pointed out is a **burlesque** on the Communist Internationale:

Arise, ye prisoners of starvation! Arise, ye slaves, no more in thrall …!"

As the chapter ends, where there has been torpid calm there is now unrest.

Historically, of course, Chapter One corresponds to the period prior to and during World War I, where Tsarism in Russia was finally, under the stress of the extraordinary demands of the war, breaking down and demonstrating that it could not work any longer. The Tsar, like Mr. Jones, was incompetent, and thus power would pass into stronger hands as power will. But as we consider the **satire** of this Chapter, it would be well to keep in mind Orwell's presentation of Major as sincere in his beliefs-for it is difficult to make a revolution without initial sincerity on the part of the leaders. Major is subtle and devious in his appeal to the animals. But he is sincere in his belief that the animals are good and deserve the fruits of their own labor, while Man is evil and robs the animals of what is rightfully theirs. Mr. Jones, (the Tsar) being absorbed only in gross pleasures and forgetful of the duties imposed on him, must be replaced. But who will replace him?

ANIMAL FARM

CHAPTER TWO

. . . .

All of the animals with the exception of Moses, the tame raven (representing the Russian Orthodox Church which was a defender of Tsarism - but ultimately used by Orwell to symbolize all institutionalized religion) had attended the meeting in the barn and heard the harangue of Major. They are all enthusiastic about the Revolution-to-be, although not being as subtle or as intelligent as Major, who had died in his sleep three days after his speech, the animals cannot perceive the fallacies of the speech. But they prepare for the revolt when the time is opportune, for Major had given the animals a completely new outlook on life, and even the dullest is no longer content with the organization of existence on Manor Farm.

The pigs, especially two who are pre-eminent among them, named Snowball and Napoleon, and a third smaller pig, Squealer, elaborate Major's teachings as expressed in his famous speech into a complete code of behavior and even a kind of system for the regulation of thought and "animal discipline." To this system they have given the name of Animalism.

The Revolution, when it comes, takes the animals by surprise; it was a spontaneous rising fostered by Mr. Jones's incompetence. He had been a good farmer, but was despondent because he had lost money in a lawsuit (Tsarist Russia's disastrous reverses during the First World War), and instead of taking corrective action Mr. Jones spends his time feeding the raven Moses on crusts of bread soaked in beer. The Revolution is precipitated by Mr. Jones's getting so drunk one week end that he forgets to feed the animals or milk the cows. The animals then spontaneously break into the feed bins and help themselves, one might say from the iron law of necessity, for they will starve if they do not do something. Rapidly they seize Manor Farm, drive out Jones, his wife, and the hired hands, smash up anything, which reminds them of the former human owners of the Farm, and paint on a wall the Seven Commandments of Animalism which had been formulated by the pigs as an "unalterable law" for the guidance of all on the Farm. Finally they change the name of the place from Manor Farm (Russia) to Animal Farm (Union of Soviet Socialist Republics), and march off to the harvest, eager to work for themselves rather than for Mr. Jones.

Comment

The Seven Commandments of Animalism, formulated by Snowball and Napoleon and the other pigs, come from the speech of Major. They are: 1. Whatever goes upon two legs is an enemy. 2. Whatever goes upon four legs, or has wings, is a friend. 3. No animal shall wear clothes. 4. No animal shall sleep in a bed. 5. No animal shall drink alcohol, 6. No animal shall kill any other animal. 7. All animals are equal.

This is the philosophy of the Revolution, and it is quite important to keep these Commandments in mind as a standard by which the progress of the Animal Farm experiment may be judged subsequently. In terms of Orwell's satiric purpose, the corruption of the Revolution from "plain living and high thinking" to more self-seeking ends on the part of some takes place in the very moment of the expulsion of Jones from the Farm. The cows are lowing even as Jones is evicted; nobody has milked them for twenty-four hours. The pigs oblige by milking them, as the pigs have found that their trotters are adaptable to such human tasks as climbing ladders or milking cows, though with some initial awkwardness. Pails of milk, five in all, are the result, and the other animals look hungrily at them. "What is going to happen to all that milk?" asks one of the animals. But Napoleon exhorts them to pay no attention to the milk but to go forward with Comrade Snowball to begin the harvest in the hayfield. The important point, which concludes this chapter, is that when the animals return from the hayfield in the evening, it was noticed that the milk had disappeared. This is the first of many such unexplained events. Pretty obviously, the pigs have disposed of the milk, either selling it or more probably at this point consuming it themselves. For while all animals are equal, the pigs have already been giving the impression that some are more equal than others.

For Orwell, this incident is indicative of his central thesis, though there is an element of humorous knavery and trickery present, as there is throughout the entire book. The central problem in human relations and human government, for Orwell, was "how to prevent power from being abused." Just as biologists have said that a biological organism begins to age and deteriorate from the first instant of its being, so a Revolution grows old and loses sight of its originally pure and idealistic motivations even in the very moment when it has come about. There will always be some group or other to pervert such a movement to its own advantage, and Orwell's **satire** uses the incident of the pigs and the milk, this early in the story of *Animal Farm,* to drive home his point. He does not say that the pigs actually took the milk; he does not need to. Much of the meaning of the book is revealed by indirection.

The Seven Commandments of Animalism have the status of revealed and unchanging law, spoken by a sort of semidivine prophet, Major. The reader will wish to observe just what happens to these Commandments. Major's wish was that the animals should not be corrupted by contact with humans or the adoption of the habits and the hankering after luxuries which characterized Mr. and Mrs. Jones and the other humans in the outside world. This may be called, using a totalitarian slogan, "revolutionary vigilance."

There are "enemies of the revolution" in the vicinity of the Farm, who wish to undo what the animals have done. One of these is Moses, the tame raven, who has told the animals of a shadowy never-never land called Sugercandy Mountain, to which animals go when they die-meanwhile, they should of course continue to work uncomplainingly for their human masters. The pigs manage to argue most of the animals out of belief in such doctrines - this is a **burlesque** of the attacks on religion by the post-revolutionary Soviet Communists. When Jones is driven off the farm, the raven goes after him flapping his wings, just as the Orthodox Church was disestablished in Russia after the downfall of the Tsar.

Mollie, a white mare ("white" as opposed to "red-though this distinction is also a bit of humorous **satire**) still hopes to be able to wear a ribbon, as she likes ribbons. Snowball cautions her after the Revolution that ribbons are the mark of human beings - they are clothing, and no animal shall wear clothes. She discards the ribbon - but is not really convinced. Ultimately Mollie will desert the animal cause and return to the society of humans, voluntarily working for them; she might be characterized as either a "right-deviationist" (one who in Communist theory veers away from "Socialist" principles in the direction of capitalism), or as a "reactionary," a "running dog of imperialism," or by various other names which are assigned to those who wish to subvert the Revolution.

While the historical **satire**, especially regarding the history of Russia subsequent to the 1917 Revolution, is open to varying interpretations, as is the history itself, several very useful studies may be mentioned here. The first is *Three Who Made a Revolution*, by Bertram D. Wolfe (1948), a biographical history of Lenin, Trotsky, and Stalin. The second is the well-known *To the Finland Station*, by Edmund Wilson (first published in 1940), which studies not only the Russian Revolution and Lenin's part in it, but the entire European tradition of revolutionary socialism, extending back for over a century. Finally, there are the biographies of Lenin and Stalin by Louis Fischer (see Bibliography below for detailed references). Fischer's *The Life of Lenin* (1964) is especially interesting for the student who wishes to learn more about the period and the men which are Orwell's concern in *Animal Farm.*

ANIMAL FARM

CHAPTER THREE

. . . .

"Although an attack on totalitarianism, *Animal Farm* is a long way from being a defense of capitalism, British or otherwise," wrote Orwell's friend and one of his biographers, Sir Richard Rees. By this Sir Richard seems to have meant that Orwell was writing here essentially on an even deeper level of **satire** than is often attributed to him in *Animal Farm,* and this thesis, which is in general adopted by the author of the present study, becomes illustrated in this chapter.

In Chapter Three, we see the archetypal pattern of decay in a new and evidently idealistic institution manifesting itself. Much work must be done on the Farm, and the animals, especially the horses (workers - the proletariat) throw themselves into the work unreservedly. The society is presumably completely classless, which is the kind of society Marx posited as the final goal of Dialectical Materialism. But even this early, the pigs seem aloof from the others. Instead of actually working, they "directed and supervised the others." They are self-appointed leaders in a society of "comrades" where there should be no leaders.

At first, the cleverness of the pigs is useful, because they can think of a way around every difficulty. Whether they are really more clever by nature, or whether they simply take upon themselves the mastery, is left ambiguous by Orwell, and this is no doubt part of his design. There is initially a high level of morality on the Farm, as all temptation to steal has ostensibly been done away with by the Revolution (Socialist Morality replacing the "bourgeois law of the jungle" in individual relationships). The "parasites" - the human beings-are gone, so that initially there is more to eat. The horse Boxer, representing the working class, has tremendously strong muscles and once he has direction as to the job to be accomplished, is a tireless and dedicated worker. Unfortunately, he does not have much ability to analyze what he is doing. His answer to every problem is a personal motto: "I will work harder!" - and the pigs are glad to take this over and make it into a slogan.

There are a few animals on the fringes who seem less than ideally happy - the cat, for instance, who has a habit of vanishing at peculiar intervals, and Old Benjamin, the donkey, who does his work exactly as he had done it under Mr. Jones, never volunteering and never doing less. But he is careful to offer no opinions on the Revolution, and the cat even outdoes him in this, for once at the beginning of the *Animal Farm* experiment when a vote was taken, the cat was found to have voted on both sides of the issue.

The pigs arrange a ceremony to take the place of Sunday religious worship; it includes the hoisting of a Flag of the Animals, a hoof and horn in white painted on an old green tablecloth.

There are debates over policy, but somehow the pigs always seem to put the resolutions. While Snowball and Napoleon are the most active in the debates, it becomes apparent that they rarely agree. Meanwhile there has been a program of education and the organization of a series of Committees, as well as the attempt to have all of the animals memorize the Seven Principles of Animalism. Since many are not capable of such an intellectual feat, Snowball declares that the Seven Commandments can be reduced to a single maxim: "Four Legs Good, Two Legs Bad." This contains the essential principle of Animalism. The sheep, for example, like it so much that they spend hours bleating it over and over. As the chapter ends, it is evident that there is strain between Napoleon and Snowball over ideology and the exercise of power.

Comment

The Revolution initially improves the lot of the animals on the Farm; after all, things could hardly have been worse than they were when Mr. Jones was the ruler. Russia under Tsarism had finally, under the extra-ordinary stresses of the First World War, ground to a halt. Under the impetus of the new order on the Farm, with the belief of the animals that they are now "working for themselves" rather than for a human exploiter, the output of the farm does improve, at least for a time. But how much may be attributed to the Revolution, Orwell asks, and how much simply to the fact of change, added to the removal of the humans?

There is already a basic difference between Snowball and Napoleon. Snowball, just as historically was the case with Leon Trotsky, is a great organizer; he forms many Committees, such as the Wild Comrades' Re-Education Committee and, for the sheep, the Whiter Wool Movement. With totalitarianism, everyone must be busy in self-criticism or in ways to increase production, in order to bring about, in Marxist theory, the "classless society" where the State will have withered away. Snowball organizes literacy classes, and these are a great success, for most of the animals by the autumn are literate to some degree, though Clover and Boxer have their difficulties. The hard-working Boxer is never able to learn the alphabet beyond, A, B, C, and D. Because he still performs prodigies of work, and is completely under the direction of the pigs, Boxer is still one of the most valuable members of the community, even though he cannot learn how to read and write. He symbolizes many who have followed various totalitarian systems blindly and sincerely, believing that the system would be their salvation and working hard on its behalf without ever thinking, or being able to think, the matter through to see the direction in which the Revolution is headed.

It should be remembered from Orwell's own biography that he believed in and hoped for a Revolution of some sort which would convert the inequality which he saw in most human societies into a state of justice and true fraternity. At the same time, Orwell saw how the motto of the French Revolution - the parent of all modern revolutions - had been departed from: "Liberty, Equality, Fraternity" could be perverted. This was the fate of all Revolutions, until men should be an awareness of actuality, of political reality and of their own natures, be able to bring about a Revolution which would not be corrupted. And the term Revolution should not cause too much uneasiness when it is applied to the state which Orwell wished to see instituted; it is more an ideological and moral change than the result of physical violence. But in this chapter, we can already see Napoleon at work seizing power for himself, undercutting his chief rival, and in general setting himself on a path which will result in the same kind of autocracy which the Farm had experienced under Jones. He ignores Snowball's Committees, and especially his plans for education. The education of the young is more important than is the attempt to educate those who are grown up and therefore are harder to change.

Napoleon takes litters of puppies from Jessie and Bluebell, and makes himself responsible for the education of the young dogs. These, through his intensive training and conditioning, will turn into a weapon he can use against the other animals; in fact, as we shall see, they correspond to the Secret Police which Stalin used to repress the population.

When there is just the beginning of grumbling over the fact that the pigs are now getting the farm's milk mixed daily into their mash, it is Squealer (the totalitarian propaganda agencies-corresponding to the Ministry of Truth in *1984)* who invents plausible reasons for such an unequal sharing of the Farm's resources. "We pigs are brainworkers," he tells the others, and assures them that it is for the sake of everyone that the pigs are to be fed better. If the pigs fail in their duty, which he fails to point out is a self-conferred duty, Jones might come back. "Surely, comrades," says Squealer, "there is no one among you who wants to see Jones come back?"

The technique of proving, or attempting to prove, a point by phrasing it as a question was much used as a rhetorical device by Stalin, as may be seen from his writings and speeches. "What is Leninism?" Stalin had asked, rhetorically, in his book Foundations of Leninism - but he already had the answer, he thought, and expounded it in the book by means of further questions and answers. (See Bibliography.) One of the chief species of enemies of the Soviet Revolution denounced by Stalin was that of the "opportunists," who would exploit a confused situation to their own advantage. Here there are obvious parallels, which Orwell no doubt intended, with the **satire** of *Animal Farm*-for Napoleon in the book has attributed to him many Stalinist characteristics, and one of the chief characteristics of Stalin was, in Orwell's view, what Stalin himself had denounced: opportunism.

As the chapter concludes, it can be seen that Snowball and Napoleon, who should be working together in the leadership of the Farm which they have assumed, are actually working at cross purposes. Something is bound to happen as a result which will affect the security of the Farm. The question is, which of the two, Snowball or Napoleon, has made provision against the day when the inevitable clash between them will come?

ANIMAL FARM

CHAPTER FOUR

. . . .

The open break, which can be seen coming, between Snowball and Napoleon, is temporarily averted by an outside threat to the new order on the Farm. The animals have been spreading the news of their Revolution to the neighboring farms by means of pigeons, who have been subverting the animals on those farms and teaching them the anthem Beasts of England. Obviously the neighbors of *Animal Farm* will not stand for this (symbolizing the fear of Bolshevism in other countries after the 1917 Revolution in Russia). If the opposition to *Animal Farm* had been strong, competent, and united, it would be a foregone conclusion that the regime of the animals would be overthrown and Mr. Jones reinstated.

Unfortunately for the anti-animal cause, the opposition is none of these. Mr. Jones has spent much of his time sitting in a tavern drinking and uttering complaints about the way he had been thrown off his own farm. But these words carry no weight, for the other farmers, however much they sympathize with him, initially do nothing. His two adjoining neighbors are Mr. Pilkington of Foxwood, an "easy-going gentleman farmer" (representing England in the historical **satire**), and Mr. Frederick of Pinchfield, a "tough, shrewd man, perpetually involved in lawsuits," (who represents the Kaiser's Germany - Frederick of Pinchfield probably having affinities with Frederick the Great of Prussia). These two are enemies, and this is lucky for the animals of the Farm, because they cannot agree even though, by having a Revolution of the animals, both Frederick and Pilkington are placed in danger.

At first, the two neighbors of Animal Farm are too busy with their own quarrel (the First World War) to pay much attention to what is going on at the Farm. They laugh the experiment to scorn. But when they see that the animals on the Farm seem to be flourishing, and when their own herds and flocks give evidence of rebellion or at least unrest, and all of the animals everywhere seem to have learned the song Beasts of England - when these things come to pass, the men finally conclude that they must take action. Only their bickering and inefficiency have saved Animal Farm so far.

One day a flock of pigeons comes to Animal Farm and warns the animals that Jones and all of his men, with reinforcements from both Foxwood and Pinchfield, are on their way to the Farm carrying weapons. But the animals have had time to make preparations, and Snowball, having read an old book on the campaigns of Julius Caesar, has organized a defense. In an **epic**, or more correctly here a comic-epic, battle, the humans are driven off after a very fierce engagement leaving dead and wounded on both sides. All take part; even the individualistic cat claws one of the humans, and the strong Boxer strikes a stable-lad from Foxwood dead with his iron-shod hoofs. Boxer is remorseful, but Snowball tells him: "War is war ... The only good human being is a dead one." Fortunately for Boxer's peace of mind, the stable-lad who had appeared dead turns out only to have been stunned. But the humans have made an ignominious retreat.

The animals have a ceremony celebrating the victory, conferring a brass medal and the title "Animal Hero, First Class," on those who had done the most for the victory: Snowball and Boxer, and posthumously the award of "Animal Hero, Second Class," on the sheep who had been killed by the men. This battle comes to be known as the Battle of the Cowshed, and holidays are established on the Farm-on October the Twelfth, to commemorate the Battle of the Cowshed, and on Midsummer Day (the Summer Solstice, June 21st) to commemorate the anniversary of the Rebellion.

Comment

The point of this chapter, in terms of the historical and political **satire**, seems to be that it is only by the incompetence, fanaticism, and bickering of the opposition that the Revolution is able to get started, and also that initially the Revolution is able to command the loyalty of the peasants, workers, and ordinary soldiers (Boxer), without whose support it would have failed immediately.

The Battle of the Cowshed corresponds to the various attacks of both internal and external enemies on the new Soviet regime. On March 3, 1918, as Germany and other countries of the Central Powers in the First World War were battling Russia, and the Germans were at the point of taking Petrograd (now Leningrad) which would have inflicted a crushing blow to the hopes of the Bolshevik government, Russia signed the Treaty of Brest-Litovsk with Germany. Thus Lenin and his associates settled temporarily with one of their enemies, though at a very high cost. The Germans insisted on very severe terms in this treaty. If they could have, they would have probably refused to conclude peace with Russia even on these terms, and would have smashed the Revolution. But the Kaiser's government, of course, wished Russia out of the war so that it could turn its full attention against the Allies on the Western Front.

In addition, there was civil war in Russia. By August 1, 1919, when the Armistice in Western Europe had already been in force for over half a year, Russia was in deep civil turmoil. White Guards (White, as opposed to Red, armies were composed of Russians loyal to Tsarims) were fighting inside Russia. But Lenin, who had appointed Leon Trotsky as Commissar of Defense, had appointed the man who could forge a revolutionary army. Trotsky is considered to be the founder of the Red Army. In addition to Russia's losses in the Treaty of Brest-Litovsk and to the civil war, there was outside intervention; in northern Russia, around Murmansk and Archangel, on the part of France and Britain; on June 11, 1918, a unit of U.S. Marines also landed at Murmansk. (Consult Fischer's *The Life of Lenin* for further information on the various interventions.)

The Russian civil war lasted nearly four years (1917-21), but in the latter year, at the cost of much hard fighting and much suffering, the last White forces were defeated. All of this history, quite complicated, still open to varying interpretations, is in part reduced to an absurdity by Orwell in the figure of the Battle of the Cowshed in *Animal Farm*. And this reduction employs a literary device of literary form used in the past for **satire**, though it is not an easy one to employ: that is mock-epic. Among great satiric writers in English, Swift, Pope, and Fielding have used this form, in which some great combat is reduced to a barnyard level (see, for example, Fielding's Tom Jones, Book IV, Chapter 8, for a "mock-battle in the Homeric style"). Orwell's **satire** has more complex qualities than Fielding's in this respect, for the Battle of the Cowshed means more than a simple dismissal of the profound importance of the fighting between the White and Red Armies during the Russian Civil War.

Probably it is best to say that Orwell singles out a few key human characteristics and translates them satirically into animal terms-without really downgrading the object of his **satire**. In this chapter, the enemies of the Revolution are shown to be incompetent, and at this point not superior ethically to the adherents of the Revolution, most of whom are still sincerely dedicated to its principles. And because the animals are still united in their support of the Revolution, while their enemies are divided, as well as incompetent and overconfident, the animals win, in defiance of probability, and thus reinforce their morale and esprit de corps. But what will now happen, Orwell asks, since the Revolution seems to have been consolidated?

ANIMAL FARM

CHAPTER FIVE

Mollie, the mare, begins to act in an old manner, and soon Clover finds occasion to speak to her on the basis of "comradely advice." Clover has seen Mollie allowing one of Mr. Pilkington's men to talk to her and stroke her nose - but Mollie denies this to Clover's face and gallops away. Investigating further ("revolutionary vigilance") Clover goes to Mollie's stall and there, under the straw, is a pile of lump sugar and several bunches of ribbons of different colors. There can be little doubt that Mollie has become a right-deviationist, a backslider, an "enemy of the people" - or should we say an enemy of the animals. Just at this time, Mollie disappears, and is later seen pulling a cart in town, gaily adorned with a scarlet ribbon. Mollie has placed herself outside the animal ranks, and is never mentioned again by her former associates.

Meanwhile, the Farm is falling on hard times after the initial successes over Mr. Jones and the "interventionists." The weather becomes bitterly cold and it is impossible to farm

(Soviet crop failures and agricultural inefficiencies in the 1920s, culminating in severe famine). The animals hold many meetings and discussions, and it becomes clear that there is a basic split between Snowball and Napoleon on almost every issue. Snowball is the better speaker at meetings, and he sways the animals to his side by his brilliant persuasiveness. But Napoleon quietly builds up machinery for rallying support, and says little. The sheep are specially his loyal supporters, and often they break into a chant of "Four legs good, two legs bad," during crucial points in Snowball's speeches.

The conflict comes to a head with a violent debate over the windmill (probably the Soviet New Economic Policy, the first Five-Year Plan, and the mechanization of agriculture). Whatever the windmill actually symbolizes, the point is that it is made the occasion of the break between Napoleon and Snowball. Snowball had proposed it as the solution to the Farm's problems; it could be harnessed to a dynamo to provide electric power, and to run various labor-saving power machinery. The animals are dumbfounded by these proposals, but Snowball is persuasive - and he has been reading books which Mr. Jones had left lying around, such as Electricity for Beginners. Snowball works furiously on the plans for the machinery, but Napoleon says little except that the windmill will not work and is a waste of time.

All the animals take sides; there are bitter factional disputes. Only Benjamin, the skeptical donkey, refuses to take sides, saying that regardless of what happens life will go on as it always has in the past-badly. At an all-Farm meeting, Napoleon and Snowball speak, respectively against and in favor of the windmill scheme. Napoleon speaks for barely thirty seconds and then indifferently sits down. Snowball launches into a brilliant oration on behalf of the windmill, and seems to be having his way, when suddenly nine enormous dogs, with brass-studded heavy collars, bound into the barn upon Napoleon's whistle. They spring at Snowball, who just has time to run out the door and, by a very close shave, outrun the dogs at his heels. The other animals are too terrified to say or do anything. Snowball disappears, and Napoleon announces that effective immediately the Sunday morning debates are cancelled. Animals will assemble on Sunday morning to salute the Animal Flag, to sing Beasts of England, and to receive their orders for the week, but debate will not be permitted. Animals who don't like the new arrangement and who might have spoken out against it are growled at by the dogs sitting around Napoleon, and find it prudent not to say anything.

Squealer goes around the Farm to explain the reason for the change to the other animals. In the spring, Napoleon announces that the windmill will be built, and while everyone is surprised at this evident reversal of his position, Napoleon has taken over Snowball's entire plan. Squealer lets it be known that Napoleon was not really opposed to the windmill; he had seemed to oppose it in order to get rid of the dangerous influence, Snowball, as a matter of "tactics." The animals are not sure what is meant by "tactics," but the dogs who happen to be accompanying Squealer growl threateningly and that does for an explanation.

Comment

It is in this chapter that the Revolution is finally seized by Napoleon, right at the end of the first half of *Animal Farm.* Force and terrorism win out over the more rational or at least verbally persuasive talents and approaches of Snowball. The fierce dogs represent Stalin's Secret Police, variously called by a succession of fearsome abbreviations: CHEKA, NKVD, OGPU, and MVD, but whatever it was called meaning, under Stalin, terrorism, repression, and "the cult of personality." The historical parallels are inexact, of course, but it bears repeating that they should not be taken too seriously. It is true that Leon Trotsky was an organizer, and was invaluable in rallying the Red Army when the new regime was reeling under both invasion and civil was just after the Russian Revolution. It is also true that Trotsky, once Stalin had consolidated his power by the use of terrorism, forced-labor, and the secret police apparatus (which the Soviets had inherited from Tsarism anyway, the Okhrana under the Tsars being the Tsarist analogue for the CHEKA, the OGPU, and other police agencies), was forced out of the Party, out of Russia into a series of residences in exile in foreign lands, and ultimately (in 1940) killed. It is thought to this day that Trotsky was assassinated in Mexico by an agent of Stalin, but this has not been conclusively established.

At any rate, at the end of the first half of *Animal Farm*, terror has outrun and bested reason and logic, and the Revolution has been captured by Napoleon. This was predictable from the slow but methodical way in which Napoleon forged a powerful following. He was also not above taking over the ideas of others, which he had formerly attacked, and making them his own; this is what he does with the plan the windmill, after denouncing Snowball for the same idea. In the perversion and twisting of the truth by Squealer we find some of the techniques which Orwell will later satirize more fully in *1984*, under the names of Doublethink and Blackwhite-deliberate distortion of reality to serve political ends. For Orwell, such techniques of "reality control" were invariable accompaniments of totalitarianism, and he attributed to Stalin the use of the techniques in full measure.

Boxer, the loyal but ignorant workhorse, adds to his slogan of "I will work harder!" a second slogan, "Napoleon is always right." If Napoleon has denounced Snowball, it must be so, says Boxer-Snowball must have been a traitor. With Snowball's expulsion, the skull of old Major had been disinterred and set up as a kind of symbol; the animals were required, after the hoisting of the Animal Flag each Sunday morning, to file past the skull in a reverent manner before entering the barn. This of course symbolizes the preservation of Lenin's body after his death in 1924 and his entombment in a glass coffin near the Kremlin, where the people could file by to look upon the founder of the Revolution. Thus, by the end of this chapter, Napoleon is firmly in control, though the logical successor to Major would have been Snowball rather than Napoleon (just as in the history of the Russian Revolution and the Soviet regime it is believed that the dying Lenin favored Trotsky over Stalin as his heir apparent, but Stalin, capturing by intrigue the Party apparatus, was able to force Trotsky out).

The second half of the book deals more with the corruption of the Animal Revolution than with the Revolution itself; it appears even more universal and less tied to history than is the first half, for in it Orwell rather pessimistically analyzes those traits of man's nature which, as he saw it, almost inevitably result in such corruption of an idealistic revolutionary principle as he believed had happened in the case of the Russian Revolution.

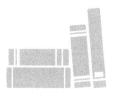

ANIMAL FARM

CHAPTER SIX

. . . .

The year after the exile of Snowball, the animals have worked like slaves; in fact, in many respects they are slaves, but they do not realize this as they believe that having driven the humans away they are working for themselves and their descendants. In addition to a sixty-hour work week, the animals are required by Napoleon to "volunteer" for work on Sundays, a typical totalitarian device where one demonstrates loyalty by doing additional unpaid work where one really has no choice in the matter.

Although the animals are working harder than ever, the results are disappointing, as the harvest is less successful than in the previous year. What is worse, the windmill presents great difficulties, although it was to have been the mainstay of the Farm's economic well-being. It is very difficult, given the limitations of the animals, to break and transport the limestone to the building site. The situation is partly saved by Boxer, who voluntarily works very long hours, repeating his two slogans:

"I will work harder," and "Napoleon is always right." Everyone admires his dedication; Boxer is careless of his own physical strength and health and spends himself in the service of the Farm. But there are still shortages of various materials on the Farm which are vital to its operation, and yet nobody has any idea how such things as nails, iron for the horses' shoes, and the machinery for the windmill can be produced on the Farm, though it is known that trade with the "outside" has been forbidden.

What happens is that Napoleon decides to engage in trade with the neighboring farms, and announces this to the animals at a Sunday meeting. There is no discussion, even though this violates the Commandments and the resolutions against the use of money or the engaging in trade with humans which the animals had passed at the time of the Revolution.

Napoleon employs a sly lawyer, a Mr. Whymper, as an intermediary between the Farm and the humans. It is even rumored that Napoleon will enter into a business deal with one of his neighbors. Worse, the pigs move into the farmhouse and out of the sty. By the winter, there have been some remarkable changes in the ordering of the Farm. But the windmill, which is now half-finished, compensates for much, and the animals are proud of it.

One morning after a raging storm in November, the animals awake to a terrible sight: the windmill, on which they had placed such hopes and on which they had made such a terrible effort is in ruins. Napoleon, looking at it, is at a loss for a moment; then he roars: "Snowball has done this thing!" He then and there pronounces a sentence of death in absentia upon Snowball, and offers a reward for his capture dead or alive. He ends with an exhortation to the animals to carry forward the work on the windmill, and to rebuild it.

Comment

The windmill **episode** probably represents historically the failure of the first Russian Five-Year Plan and the equal failure of a modified economic system (The New Economic Policy, promulgated by Lenin in 1921). Further, it was in 1921 that Lenin, seeing that Russia would need to obtain certain essential materials from the outside world by trade, entered into negotiations with representatives of various foreign countries to establish trade relations. This seemed a reversal of previous policy when the Soviet regime, which, after all, had been fighting against many of the Western countries which had supported the White forces, would then trade with the same countries which had been the enemy. But it was necessary to do this - to establish trade, for Russia could not be an independent economy at this time - and Lenin recommended the step, at the Tenth Party Congress. Russia's nationalized industries had, under the stress of war and revolution, seriously deteriorated, and famine was in the land. Departing temporarily from Marxist ideology, Russia began to enter into trade with outside capitalists.

Orwell, of course, compresses many historical occurrences into this chapter. The essential point is that conditions on the Farm require modification of the former revolutionary principles, and this modification comes about in a very sly manner, which the ordinary workers, the rank and file, only dimly perceive because they have been too busy performing heavy physical labor-like Boxer especially-to notice how the changes are taking place. "Napoleon is always right," says Boxer, and even if the animals rather distrust Napoleon and fear him and his following of fierce dogs, they do trust Boxer who, because of his strength, dedication and willingness to work enjoys the highest prestige among them.

The Seven Commandments of Animalism are being changed by the pigs, very quietly, in this chapter. After the pigs move into the house, the other animals remember that the Fourth Commandment is: "No animal shall sleep in a bed." Some of them, Clover for instance, are curious. Clover, unable to read the Commandments herself, brings Muriel, who spells it out: "No animal shall sleep in a bed with sheets." Clover, whose memory was not of the best, had not remembered that the Commandment said anything about sheets, but it must be so if Muriel sees it in writing. At the same time Squealer arrives with some dogs to "explain" the matter. The pigs, he tells them, are brainworkers and therefore for the good of the Farm need the rest provided by the beds. The sheets, on the other hand, which are a human invention, are prohibited. By casuistry, an accompaniment of totalitarian propaganda, Squealer "proves" that the pigs are justified in living in the house and in arising an hour later than the others. Here Orwell is probably thinking more of Nazi propaganda-of the Big Lie, the dictum put into practice by Hitler and by his sinister Propaganda Minister, Dr. Goebbels-for Hitler and Goebbels believed that if a lie were repeated often and emphatically enough it would be accepted as true by the unthinking people. So Squealer convinces even the reluctant, with terror (the dogs) always at his side as a final "persuader." As the chapter ends, Napoleon has created a scapegoat, Snowball, for the shortcomings of his regime, as totalitarians must do, said Orwell.

ANIMAL FARM

CHAPTER SEVEN

The Farm now has its scapegoat, to whom all the shortcomings of the program are attributed. Snowball, who had once been a hero among the animals, is now an exiled and hunted malefactor. He becomes the occasion for the action in this chapter, which is perhaps the most brilliant of all in *Animal Farm* in terms of its satiric effect.

The Farm is very short on food and supplies that winter. Napoleon's plan is to distract the inhabitants of the Farm from these shortages, due in large measure to inefficiency and a defective production and distribution system, and to distract them by finding someone on whom he can blame everything. He defines Snowball as a traitor who has been in league at different times both with Mr. Pilkington and Mr. Frederick. Meanwhile he has a revolt on his hands. Napoleon had concealed the shortage of food from his human agent, Mr. Whymper, but he negotiates through the lawyer a contract to sell four hundred eggs a week to the "outside." This, if fulfilled, will keep the Farm going that winter. The hens revolt against this, but Napoleon ruthlessly suppresses the rebellion. Then, calling together the animals, he says that there are traitors and agents of Snowball in their midst. A number of animals, to everyone's amazement, denounce themselves and confess to a variety of high crimes and misdemeanors, whereupon they are immediately executed by the fierce dogs. Blood flows freely, and the survivors are both terrified and cowed. Some of them remember the Sixth Commandment: "No animal shall kill any other animal." But this seems to have been forgotten in practice if not in theory, under the need to exterminate the "saboteurs and traitors." As the chapter ends, Napoleon has prohibited even the singing of Beasts of England, and has substituted instead a much more innocuous and unmelodic anthem composed by Minimus, the poet.

Comment

Historically this chapter compresses and gives perspective to a period of nearly twenty years of Soviet-style Communist government, and it is obvious that Orwell had this in mind when he wrote this part of *Animal Farm;* he had made reference to it in other writings, and was to use it again in *1984.* The period begins with the failure of the Soviet regime's economic policies in the 1920s and the famine which was the result. But the major part of this sequence of events has to do with the amazing series of Soviet purge trials of the 1930s.

The purges were incredible; they shocked the world, for never had anything quite like them been seen. Accompanying them were the famous "show trials," for there were five great trials, held in Moscow between August 1936 and March 1938, in which a number of high-ranking Soviet leaders were accused of treacherous acts against the State, convicted, and most of them executed. But the truly remarkable thing about the trials was the willingness of the defendants to confess. As former Soviet Premier N. S. Krushchev himself is alleged to have said, in a secret speech in February, 1956, in the course of which he denounced Stalin's crimes and his "cult of personality", the defendants in the Moscow purge trials were, "against all norms of current legal science," convicted almost entirely on the basis of their own unsupported confessions. And it was later proven that by a complex series of techniques involving medicine, psychology, and other disciplines, as well as sheer physical torture, the defendants were brought to such a physical and psychological condition that they would freely in open court confess their "crimes against the State," whether or not they had actually committed the acts which they were charged with.

An interesting and useful book on this subject is *From Purge to Coexistence*, by David J. Dallin (Chicago: Henry Regnery Co., 1964), though it concentrates more on the history than on the interestingly bizarre psychology behind the Moscow Trials. A more famous work, written after the Trials during the period 1939-40 by Arthur Koestler, is *Darkness at Noon,* in which a fictional character, based on several of the actual defendants, one N. S. Rubashov, is tortured, tried, confesses, is convicted by the Supreme Revolutionary Court of Justice, sentenced to death, and shot, as was often the custom in these cases, in the cellars of the Secret Police.

What is important in considering this section of *Animal Farm* is Orwell's obsession with the needs of a totalitarian state which is not satisfied with simple physical obedience; it must have loyalty so intense that even the condemned traitors will be their own accusers. Orwell was to develop this **theme** much more elaborately in *1984,* because roughly half of that famous work deals with a confrontation between torturer and tortured ending in the destruction, and the full confession and return to commitment to Big Brother, of Winston Smith, the hero of *1984*. Orwell depicts in *1984* the techniques of brainwashing in great detail, showing how man is thereby reduced to the level of an animal and robbed of all freedom and human dignity by the all-powerful totalitarian state. In *Animal Farm,* in Chapter Seven especially, he treated the subject from quite a different perspective than was the case later in *1984.* He reduced it to its simplest level, in the barnyard, and stripping away all the tortuous reverse logic of the trials and the brainwashing (many of whose victims, after a shift in Party orientation, were posthumously "rehabilitated" after they had been executed) Orwell showed naked lust for power, insane suspiciousness, and the blackest double-dealing at work. Yet even here, in an area which moved him deeply, Orwell was able to retain the light touch, and he did not allow his vehemence on the subject of brainwashing and torture to get the better of him and to make him lose the thread of his satiric animal fable. The animals, in their puzzlement, are more lifelike than life. That they had come to this: the floor of the barn covered with the blood of their own comrades, executed by the agents of Napoleon! It is hard for Boxer and the others to believe, and the animals are "shaken and miserable" as the chapter ends. But they must believe what Napoleon has told them about Snowball and his traitorous followers on the Farm; besides, they have no choice but to believe, in view of the powerful guards and the propaganda agency of Squealer with which Napoleon has surrounded himself. The abolition of Beasts of England signifies the death of the Revolution and its replacement by a police state, whatever Napoleon chooses to call it.

ANIMAL FARM

CHAPTER EIGHT

· ·

After the terror inspired by the public confessions and executions had died down somewhat, several of the animals remembered, or thought they remembered, the wording of the Sixth Commandment: "No animal shall kill any other animal." This seems very clear even to the dullest mind, and it is further observed that the executions somehow violate this Commandment. Clover once again, being herself unable to read well, asks Muriel to read her the Sixth Commandment. And Muriel reads: "No animal shall kill any other animal without cause."

While the animals do not remember the additional two words, "without cause," since they are written they must be so. Since those who had been executed had given cause by being traitors, it followed that they were justly executed according to the Commandment. Meanwhile, the animals work all that year to rebuild the windmill. Napoleon is more distant and more grandiose than ever, traveling around the farm escorted by the guard of dogs, keeping himself in lofty isolation from the others, and being addressed formally as "our Leader, Comrade Napoleon." The animals outdo each other in fulsome praise of Napoleon and his outstanding ability and wisdom in all fields of endeavor. In fact, a hymn praising Napoleon is composed by Minimus, the Poet.

Napoleon engages in complicated negotiations with Frederick of Pinchfield and Pilkington of Foxwood. At first Napoleon leans toward Pilkington, for the animals are more afraid of Frederick, who is believed to be far more brutal in his treatment of animals. The windmill is finished. Suddenly Napoleon veers toward Frederick and agrees to sell him some timber. But the money which Frederick pays for the lumber turns out to be counterfeit, and in the same moment as the animals find out this deception, Frederick attacks the Farm and dynamites the new windmill; a terrible disaster for Animal Farm, for this is the second time the windmill has been destroyed. The invading forces of Frederick are driven off at heavy cost, but the mill is totally destroyed. Napoleon converts the occurrence into a victory, which he and his associates celebrate by getting drunk, and having a wild party in the farmhouse which is barely concealed from the "common people" - the citizenry of the Farm. Yes, the Fifth Commandment had said, the animals thought: "No animal shall drink alcohol." But actually, as Muriel points out when she reads it again, the wording is: "No animal shall drink alcohol to excess."

Comment

The changing of the wording of the Commandments is done secretly, though in this chapter Squealer is nearly caught in the act of doing this when he falls from a ladder in the dead of night near the wall on which the Commandments are inscribed. A paint pot is seen by the animals who rush to the place where Squealer is lying stunned beside the broken ladder, but the dogs immediately make a ring around him and escort him back to the farmhouse. The onlookers cannot quite figure the meaning of this out, so Squealer escapes discovery. What is signified by this incident as well as by the covertly changed wording of one Commandment after another is the process used by totalitarian states which Orwell was to call "Doublethink" or Reality Control in *1984*. It is a process whereby the idea that there can be any objective and unchanging truth is negated; the truth is whatever the Party or the Leader say it is at the moment. Orwell wrote, in his essay "Politics and the English Language," that this idea - the relativity and changeability of truth - bothered him more than bombs or bayonets.

Stalin's followers in other countries just prior to the German attack on Russia were hard put to justify the shifts in position of the Soviet Government in the period 1938-41, in which Stalin concluded a non-aggression pact with Hitler. The pact evidently was as worthless as the counterfeit bank notes with which Frederick of Pinchbeck paid Napoleon for the lumber, which is what Orwell meant to signify by the transaction in the historical satire of *Animal Farm*. The Nazi-Soviet pact shocked the friends and admirers of the Soviets perhaps more than any other single incident in the time since the Russian Revolution. The climactic purge trials of 1937, in which eight high-ranking leaders of the Russian Army, including the revolutionary war hero Marshal Mikhail Tukhachevsky and seven other generals were tried, did not look well to the outside world either, especially when all eight were accused of an attempt "to help restore in the U.S.S.R. the role of landlords and capitalists." All eight were executed, and it has been said that Stalin, by purging most of the top officers of the Russian Army and throwing the rest into a state of confusion and fear just prior to the attack planned by Hitler, was indirectly responsible for the initial German successes against Russia in 1941. Orwell reduces all this to the barnyard where, he implies, it belonged.

There are certain details in the **satire** of Chapter Eight which bear additional comment. Napoleon has ordered the propaganda-carrying pigeons (the Comintern, or Stalinist agency for spreading revolution into other countries) to stay away from Foxwood, when Napoleon was negotiating with Pilkington of Foxwood for the sale of the lumber. But then Napoleon had a change of mind, and throws his attention to Frederick-just as Stalin had cultivated the English, then switched to Hitler, and then (double-crossed by the Nazis in June, 1941, with the German Panzer attack on Russia), had loudly called for and received help from England.

Another aspect of the **satire** here is the rewriting of history, which Orwell will treat in more detail in *1984*. Snowball had been awarded the medal of "Animal Hero, First Class," after the Battle of the Cowshed long ago. Gradually this had become, in the minds of the animals, artfully informed by Napoleon through Squealer, the title "Animal Hero, Second Class." But even this is taken away from Snowball, and in this chapter Napoleon proclaims that Snowball had been a traitor from the very beginning.

The Battle of the Windmill, which destroys most of what the Farm has built up since the Revolution, corresponds of course to the Nazi attack on Russia. It is not so much Napoleon's screams and exhortations as a more primitive feeling for the land and the Farm which makes the animals, especially that tower of strength, Boxer, fight so valiantly for the Farm. Just as the Germans, as they advanced into the heart of Russia, alienated the people by brutal treatment and aroused a desire to see them thrown right out, so Frederick of Pinchfield, by his destruction of the windmill, hits the animals hard - but they are still determined to recover. During the Second World War, the revolutionary aspect of Communism - the emphasis on world-revolution and the class-struggle - was held somewhat in abeyance by Stalin, because he did not want to risk alienating Britain and America, who were supplying him with vast quantities of war materials. Orwell represents this, as has been pointed out, by the instructions to the pigeons given by Napoleon. The drunken party and the setting up of a winery at the end of this chapter represent the special privileges which the leaders of Animal Farm have assumed with no authority from the "comrades." So it is, implies Orwell, and so it will always be, that once a revolution is made and leaders get into power, they will be corrupted and will seek special privileges.

ANIMAL FARM

CHAPTER NINE

Now the animals work furiously again, although the older generation of Old Revolutionaries, such as Boxer, is somewhat worn down. Some are at or near the age of comfortable retirement which had been established when Jones had been driven out. Of course, no animal had actually retired and received a pension, but there had been lean years where much work had to be done to consolidate the Animal Revolution.

Meanwhile, another hard winter comes, and even though Squealer is always ready to recite lists of production "victories," still the fact is that rations are once more reduced, except for the rations of the pigs, and their guards and auxiliaries, the dogs. The Farm does slightly better economically, however, though the shortages of food remain. Spontaneous Demonstrations, in which the animals are ordered to participate, are held, with processions and colored shirts and the chanting of the sheep who are Napoleon's greatest devotees. Animal Farm, the April following the attack of Frederick's men, is proclaimed a Republic and a President is elected, but Napoleon is the only candidate and he is elected unanimously. Meanwhile, Moses gives out more information about the Sugarcandy Mountains, and Napoleon and Squealer release more documents about Snowball's treasonable activities; the papers "prove" him to have been on the side of the humans from the very beginning of the Revolution. By now the animals, even those who knew Snowball well at the time of the Revolution, have only dim memories of him and believe what they are told, especially since it would be quite dangerous for them not to believe what Comrade Napoleon says.

Boxer, who has spent his strength in the service of the Farm and who has been one of the mainstays of Napoleon's regime, more through loyalty to the Farm than through loyalty to Napoleon, has suffered a breakdown in health. His lungs are weakening after the years of hard labor. He had been looking forward to retirement, but when he collapses, Squealer calls an "ambulance." In the middle of the day, when the other animals are at work, it comes. Benjamin, who can read, is terrified; this is the first time anyone can remember seeing him so disturbed. He reads aloud to the other animals what is written on the side of the "ambulance": "Alfred Simmonds, Horse Slaughterer and Glue Boiler, Willingdon. Dealer in Hides and Bonemeal."

Boxer is being taken to the knacker's to be made into glue and meal; this is the grisly truth. So Napoleon rewards those who have been faithful to him. Boxer is said to have died in the hospital, his last words being "Napoleon is always right." And just coincidentally, that same night the pigs, having obtained money from some unexplained source, purchase a case of whiskey and engage in a drunken party capped by a tremendous brawl amongst them, which is kept quiet from the other animals.

Comment

Stalin had "liquidated" many of his enemies and supposed enemies, the trial of Marshal Tukhachevsky in 1937, referred to in Chapter Eight, perhaps being a historical analogue to the **episode** of Boxer. What Orwell means to say here satirically is simply the indifference, as he saw it, of all totalitarian regimes to those who serve them faithfully, and the ingratitude and vanity of dictators represented by Napoleon.

Boxer had trusted Napoleon up to the last moment, but then he must have learned the truth: and to Orwell the betrayal of one's ideals was similar to death: it was death, because to rob one of an ideal to which he has committed his life is a dreadful thing. Orwell himself believed that he had passed beyond the stage of seeing the world through a cloud of illusion, through rose-colored spectacles. The incident of Boxer is all too possible Orwell is saying; in fact it is the rule when one serves corrupt masters.

Squealer, here representing perhaps the totalitarian State-controlled press, is ready to give out limitless explanations of what is going on: lists of produced goods and indexes showing that the animals have a much higher standard of living than they ever did under Jones. But no matter how encouraging the lists are, the animals, other than the pigs and dogs, are still short of food. One class of exploiters has simply been replaced by another; the ordinary inhabitants of the Farm, Orwell says, have seen little or no improvement in their lot-with the added depressing fact that Napoleon and his minions are much more efficient in the long run than was the drunken and incompetent Farmer Jones. Squealer also uses euphemisms: "readjustment," for "reduction." of the daily ration. Even "ambulance" for "horse -

slaughterer's van" is a grim jest. This point is greatly expanded in *1984*, in which the new language, Newspeak, is calculated to confuse the gullible with euphemism and understatement. Orwell gave the definitive statement of his views on the matter of political decay leading to the corruption of language in his essay "Politics and the English Language" (1946), written just about the time he was finishing *Animal Farm* or a little later, but stemming from the same preoccupations.

Class-distinctions are now introduced on the Farm, although in theory the society was a "classless society" as Marx had posited would be the case under Communism. Small distinctions are magnified: animals meeting one of the pigs on a narrow path are required to stand aside. And the pigs are granted the privilege of wearing green ribbons on their tails on Sundays. All class distinctions had been done away with at the Revolution: "All animals are equal" was a principle promulgated as the Seventh and Last Commandment of the Principles of Animalism. But somehow the green ribbons and the gestures of subservience to the pigs and especially to Comrade Napoleon do not square; with this Commandment, as even the less intelligent animals perceive. Finally, the Spontaneous Demonstrations are a trapping of totalitarianism; one knows of course that they are carefully organized and disciplined because a totalitarian Leader, while he needs these wild manifestations of popular support and hero-worship, cannot afford to have such things getting out of hand. But under Napoleon there is not fear of this on Animal Farm.

It is very strange to the animals that Moses, with his story of the Sugarcandy mountains awaiting them after death, is tolerated by the pigs, who even supply him with a ration of beer although he is not required to do physical work. Orwell interpreted the return of the Church - the Russian Orthodox

Church - after the Revolution as a belief on the part of the authorities that if the Church made people content with their lot in this life it did not matter that in theory it was opposed to Communism. In the **satire** of *Animal Farm,* therefore, Moses is simply another agency, along with the terrorism of Napoleon-trained Secret Police, the dogs, for keeping the citizenry quiet.

As the chapter ends, very few of the "old guard," the original revolutionaries, are left and the memories of those who remain are dimmed with time. Napoleon may thus feel safe in making his final move.

ANIMAL FARM

CHAPTER TEN

There are many new inhabitants of the Farm now, none of whom can remember the Revolution. The Farm is run more efficiently, and the windmill had been rebuilt and is used not for electric power but for milling corn. But a second is to be built (accelerating the industrialization of the Farm). Ordinary animals work just as hard as ever, as Napoleon had said that vacations and heated and lighted stalls were "contrary to the spirit of Animalism." While the Farm seems richer, the ordinary animals are no richer - the surplus wealth seems to go into the hands of the pigs and dogs, just as in the old days it went to Mr. Jones. But the greatest shock is to come.

One day the animals see a sight frightening in the extreme: a pig, Squealer, walking on his hind legs. Soon all of the pigs appear from the farmhouse, walking in this manner. And then Napoleon appears, on two legs and carrying a whip. The sheep begin bleating: "Four legs good, two legs better!" No other animal dares to say anything. As this seems such a radical departure from Animalism, Clover asks Benjamin to take her to the end of the big barn where on the wall the Commandments are written. But instead of the Seven Commandments, all that Benjamin sees written on the wall is this:

All Animals Are Equal But Some Animals Are More Equal Than Others

This, then, is what has become of the spirit of the Revolution. It is predictable that shortly thereafter the neighboring farmers come at Napoleon's invitation to a banquet to see the Farm for themselves. Peering in at the festivities, the ordinary animals of the Farm see Napoleon, Mr. Pilkington, and other assorted pigs and humans, who suddenly begin quarreling violently. But it is impossible for the onlookers to say which of those who are quarreling are men and which are pigs.

Comment

In this last chapter, Orwell shows us that the wheel has come full circle, and the regime which has been set up by the pigs in the name of the Animal Revolution is at least as bad, if not worse, as the regime under Jones. It is more efficient, it is true, because Jones was so undisciplined and pleasure-loving (he had died in a home for inebriates years after his expulsion from the Farm) that he could not run the Farm especially when it was under the extraordinary stress of war or a series of bad harvests. And technology had advanced in the meantime, but it is hard to establish whether the pigs could really take much credit for this; the original idea for the windmill had been Snowball's although Napoleon took it over for himself.

All of the Commandments had been rewritten, until finally they are compressed into one: the most famous line in *Animal Farm* and a perfect summation of Orwell's satiric **theme** and purpose:

All Animals Are Equal But Some Animals Are More Equal Than Others.

Pilkington of Foxwood represents England; even though ostensibly the Farm itself is located in England it actually represents Russia in the terms of Orwell's satiric fable. England, as was the case with most other countries, had been deeply suspicious of the Soviet experiment. By the banquet at which Pilkington and his associates were the guests of the ruler of the Farm, Orwell meant to signify England's cooperation with Stalin during the Second World War, though of course England's interests were served during this cooperation. But at the banquet, probably symbolizing the defeat of Germany, which occurred just as Orwell finished writing the conclusion of *Animal Farm,* it could already be discerned by some that there was likely to be a conflict of interest between Russia and the Western Allies. Russia had been idealized by many outsiders during the War, because of the tremendous battle which it put up against the invading armies of Hitler-it was believed by many that the character of the Stalinist regime had basically changed. Thus the speech made at the banquet by Napoleon shows "gratitude" for the "misapprehensions" about the Farm having been corrected. They did not seek to spread revolutionary doctrines, but just wished to attend to their own business and be good neighbors. Thus both humans and animals can drink a toast: "To the prosperity of Animal Farm!"

Napoleon, in replying to the toast, says that his animals (workers) do more work for less pay than do any workers on other farms, and the humans say that there are many things in Napoleon's system which they would like to emulate. The title of "Comrade" has been abolished by Napoleon.

But just at the end, as the animals who are now the slaves of Napoleon creep away from their eavesdropping on the great banquet, they hear a quarrel and harsh words. Napoleon and Pilkington have been playing at cards - the cooperation of Russia and the West during the Second World War. But now each accuses the other of playing the ace of spades simultaneously, and as there is only one ace of spades (world domination) they cannot both have it; so as the book ends the humans and the animals, looking very much like each other despite their alleged difference of species, have fallen to quarreling again, as both desire a thing which only one can have and which, in Orwell's view, nobody should have.

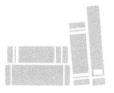

ANIMAL FARM

· ·

Farmer Jones

Specifically he represents the last Russian Tsar, Nicholas II, generally he represents the Tsarist system which had gradually broken down in Russia as it was unable to adjust to changing social and economic conditions. At the most fundamental level Jones represents the breakdown of the old European monarchist order in most countries - "the decay of ability in the ruling class," as Orwell had put it in another essay of his.

Jones is incompetent and selfish; instead of running the farm efficiently he sometimes becomes so drunk that he forgets about his care of the animals who, after all, are his very livelihood. When there is a power-vacuum, something will happen to fill it. Jones is driven off the Farm by a truly spontaneous rising of the hungry animals, who would not have risen at all even after being exposed to the harangue of Old Major had it not been for the fact that Jones came home drunk one week end and just callously forgot about milking the cows and about his other duties. So Jones is by no means a hero. Orwell implies that perhaps he would have been even more of a capricious tyrant except for his drunkenness and consequent inefficiency. And while Napoleon will ultimately adopt the same vice as Jones, at least his drinking is kept fairly secret and he does not allow it to interfere very much with his efficiency as a dictator.

Napoleon

Really the central character of *Animal Farm,* if we accept the interpretation of the book as being a **satire** on totalitarianism. It is probable that Orwell chose the name for his central and prime dictatorial figure because Napoleon himself, the historical Napoleon, Emperor of the French, became the Leader only a few years after the hopes for Liberty, Equality, Fraternity, and the Rights of Man had been embodied in the French Revolution. Yet from the Revolution, in which the people expelled the aristocracy of the old regime and executed their King, to the point where Napoleon assumed the title of Emperor and became as autocratic as - and much more efficient than - the former King of France, was only a period of fifteen years; Napoleon having become First Consul ten years after the Revolution and Emperor of the French five years later. And such was the fate of all Revolutions - this is one of Orwell's master themes. Power corrupts, and the pig-Napoleon who figures so prominently in *Animal Farm* is just repeating a pattern.

Napoleon of *Animal Farm,* like Stalin, is presented as slower than his arch-rival Snowball (Trotsky). He is not particularly creative in ideas, but he does know when to take over an idea from someone else, such as Snowball's plan for the windmill, and make it his own. And he knows how to build an apparatus for controlling others, as did Stalin. He uses assistants, such as

Squealer, who may be more clever than he is - but he knows their limitations and how to keep them in line. Napoleon is characterized by great force of will and personality, total lack of scruples (as witness his shameful treatment of the faithful Boxer), and some uncontrolled personal habits which he is careful to keep out of sight of the masses, though his trusted followers who are dependent on his good will know about them.

Snowball

The rival of Napoleon; a boar who is more clever than Napoleon, much more creative and inventive, but who lacks "staying power" and the kind of ability for intrigue which would have enabled him to build a powerful machine for the domination of the Farm. As pointed out in the text, he would seem to be Trotsky in terms of the historical **satire** on Russian history. But he represents also the scapegoat, needed by every dictator. The Leader claims to be omnipotent and all-powerful; how then can he have failures, such as the terrible fiasco of the dynamiting of the windmill by Frederick's men and the payment for the timber in counterfeit notes which Napoleon foolishly accepted? To admit that this was the Leader's fault would be to weaken his position. Therefore, Napoleon blames everything on Snowball, the arch villain. The credulous animals believe him, as their memories are not of the best - and those who do not believe what Napoleon said about Snowball find it prudent to keep these opinions to themselves. Everything which goes wrong on the Farm is blamed on Snowball, and Napoleon thus succeeds in creating a "devil," an adversary to satisfy the psychological need of his subjects to have an object on whom they may project their frustration at the failure of some of the programs of the Farm.

Old Major

The prophet of the Animal Revolution, who dies before the Revolution actually takes place. An idealist, a law-giver, and a spellbinding orator, he puts the idea of rebellion into the heads of the animals with a clever appeal backed by probable sincerity. Old Major, a majestic-looking pig twelve years old (an advanced age for a pig), has a wise and benevolent appearance, though his tushes have never been cut and look quite formidable and dangerous-as are his ideas. His is the dream of the Revolution, and he seems to represent Karl Marx, the most important historical theoretician of Communism and of the doctrine of world revolution which is to bring about a millennial and classless society and to change human nature. It is important to an understanding of Orwell's **satire** that he presents Old Major as a sincere dreamer, an "idea man" (idea pig, more accurately), who of necessity will leave to others the task of carrying out the Revolution. And others will corrupt the original ideas of Old Major, as always happens, Orwell implies, in a shift of power or a revolution.

Old Major seems to represent V. I. Lenin as well as Karl Marx, as his successors are Napoleon and Snowball, who fight over the succession to power with the result that Snowball loses and is exiled. But Stalin and Trotsky were successors not to Marx directly, but to Lenin; and therefore Old Major, in the historical **satire**, has the dual meaning. On the fundamental, even archetypal level, Old Major represents all great thinkers, even religious as well as political leaders, who have changed the conditions of life with their ideas, even as their ideas were taken over by followers, sometimes too ambitious followers, who perverted these ideas to their own advantage and to the enslavement and oppression of the masses. Old Major, then, though he appears only briefly in the first chapter of *Animal Farm*, is a very important character.

Squealer

The "mouthpiece" of Napoleon, corresponding to a totalitarian minister of propaganda such as Dr. Goebbels under Hitler. He makes the worse appear the better reason, and is always ready with lists of figures showing that the animals were constantly becoming better off than they had been the year before, and in any case were better off than under Jones.

Squealer does much of Napoleon's dirty work, and it is clear that he exercises "reality control" over the other, less perceptive or subtle, animals. Squealer was once nearly caught in the act. The Commandments painted on the barn seemed to change, to have words added and deleted, and one night after a drunken carouse in the farmhouse, Squealer was found insensible under the place where the Commandments were painted, a broken ladder and a paint pot nearby. But the dogs surrounded him and led him off, so the animals did not suspect the truth, or if they did they kept quiet about it. Squealer has the function of concealing the truth from the animals, and in doing so he perverts even the language, using euphemisms instead of plain words to make that which is brutal or treacherous palatable. Squealer ultimately becomes so fat that he has difficulty seeing-for he is very well fed, in contrast to the ordinary workers on the arm.

The Dogs

A group of fierce hounds which Napoleon had trained up himself as his own guards, taking them under his protection at an early age. They corresponded to the Secret Police and to the other apparatus of terrorism and repression in a totalitarian state.

Mr. Pilkington Of Foxwood

One of the two closest neighbors to Animal Farm. Foxwood is a large but rather neglected farm, rather overgrown by woodland. Mr. Pilkington is an easygoing gentleman who does not have quite the vices of Jones but who spends much time hunting and fishing. Pilkington of Foxwood represents England, or at any rate the British Government. At the end of the book Pilkington cooperates with Napoleon, but then they have a severe quarrel, corresponding to the widening split between Stalin, who wanted to seize as much of Europe as possible, and the Western Allies which began to develop even as the military defeat of Germany was being concluded.

Mr. Frederick Of Pinchfield

Corresponding to the German nation, Frederick is tough and shrewd and quarrelsome in Orwell's view: he is always involved in lawsuits (wars) and drives hand bargains. Pinchfield is a smaller but better-kept and more efficiently run farm than is Foxwood. Frederick makes an agreement to buy some timber from Napoleon, which corresponds to the Russo-German nonaggression pact before the Second World War - but then he totally double-crosses Napoleon by paying for the timber in counterfeit notes and at the same time attacks Animal Farm and dynamites the windmill on which the animals had lavished such effort. But the ordinary citizens of the Farm, inspired by the strength of Boxer, rally and drive Frederick off.

Mr. Whymper

An attorney, hired by Napoleon as intermediary between the Farm and the humans on the "outside." He represents the middleman, the necessary business relationships which must take place even between states which are hostile to one another, and in the process he seems slyly to enrich himself. The animals do not trust him, but on the other hand their egos are fed by seeing a human, one of their former masters, serving them.

Moses

A raven, who does not work as the other animals do on the Farm. Originally Mr. Jones's especial pet, he is a spy and talebearer. He tries to make the animals resigned to their lot by telling them of a mysterious country called Sugarcandy Mountain where all animals go when they die. Some of the animals even believed these stories. When Jones is forced to flee, Moses follows him, but in due time reappears on the Farm and is, strangely, accepted by the pigs and given a ration to support him even though he still does no work. The pigs find him a useful ally, because the story of the Sugarcandy Mountains keeps the animals quiet, or helps to do so. He symbolizes, in Orwell's **satire**, the Orthodox Church.

Benjamin

The donkey, a cynic who does not believe that anything will be different once the Revolution has come. He is the oldest animal on the farm, and has the worst temper; he is never seen to laugh. If asked why, he says that he sees nothing to laugh at. However, he works hard though he is a "loner," and he is devoted to Boxer, whose strength and dedication he respects. He tries to save Boxer near the end, when Boxer is hauled off to the knacker in a van - but he is unsuccessful in this. His pessimistic view about the outcome of the Revolution corresponds in some particulars to Orwell's own view.

Boxer

An enormously strong horse, who performs prodigies of physical strength. He is not very bright, and is ultimately tricked to his death by Napoleon once his strength has given out in the service of Animal Farm. He believes in the Revolution, and coins two personal slogans; "I will work harder," and "Comrade Napoleon is always right." He fights bravely during the Battle of the Cowshed, and Napoleon's treatment of him is the blackest ingratitude. He represents the unthinking masses; he is really loyal more to the Farm than to Napoleon, but he is not clever enough to protect himself against Napoleon.

Clover

A mare, also a hard worker, not very bright, who like Boxer allows herself to be tricked again and again by the pigs. She knows dimly that things have not worked out quite in the way that the Revolution had promised, but she cannot perceive why. Clover, too, is Boxer's friend and tries to save him from his fate.

Muriel

A white goat, who is able to read somewhat better than most of the animals and reads the Commandments for them.

Mollie

A pleasure-loving white mare who draws Mr. Jones's trap; she succumbs to the attractions of "bourgeois society", and would probably be called a "reactionary" or a "right-deviationist."

The Cat

An individualist, who votes on both sides of the question raised at the meeting with Old Major, and who has no commitment to either side.

The Sheep

The mindless masses, who can only bleat slogans in support of Comrade Napoleon.

Bluebell, Jessie, And Pincher

Three dogs, whose puppies are taken by Napoleon at an early age and "conditioned" so that he may make of them his guards and Secret Police.

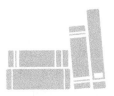

ANIMAL FARM

In World Review (June 1950), Mr. T. Hopkinson, reviewing and re-evaluating *Animal Farm,* said that it was one of the two modern books, or at any rate works of fiction, before which the critic must abdicate. By that is meant that the book simply speaks for itself; it has own force and logic. The other book which Hopkinson singled out was Koestler's *Darkness at Noon.* To these he might have added a third: *1984.*

Orwell held before himself an ideal of clear and concise writing, open to only a minimum of misinterpretation and misconstruction. For, he said in the essay "Politics and the English Language," much writing was simply words gummed together with little or no meaning-or worse, intended to confuse the reader and to blind him to what was actually going on. With corruption in politics and government, Orwell observed, as had his master Jonathan Swift before him, comes corruption in language; a blunting of the edges of words and a dulling of their meaning. It may be said that in his two masterpieces, *Animal Farm* and *1984,* he lived up to this ideal so well that critics have been left with relatively little to say about the books other than to praise them for their honesty and for their artistic merit.

Even interpretation and explication of the texts is of less utility, apparently, than is the case with criticism of most of the great American and European novelists of the twentieth century, while it is perhaps not accurate to say, with John Atkins: "All the useful things that can be said about *Animal Farm* at this early stage have already been said. Perhaps, three hundred years later, critics will find hidden significances which we cannot grasp as contemporaries, just as *Gulliver's Travels* continues to yield its meanings, some of them having been elucidated by Orwell himself," - still, the interpretation of *Animal Farm* at present seems fairly clear.

At the time of the writing of this present guide, it can be said that there has been no definitive critical biography or critical study of George Orwell. The most elaborate studies of Orwell available, each of which contains some material on *Animal Farm* commented on separately below, are books by John Atkins, Christopher Hollis, and Richard Rees. The latter two writers were personal acquaintances of Orwell, and their books contain firsthand reminiscences of some value which will no doubt assist in the writing of a definitive study someday. Perhaps we have been too close to Orwell, since his death a decade and a half ago, to have the kind of perspective which leads to a major work of criticism being written about him. So far the criticism is potential, not actual. Yet he is an important writer; perhaps the major English writer of the 1940s and early 1950s, though this is an extreme claim to make. His place in literary history today is by no means settled, and there are good reasons why this should be so.

For in considering the ultimate reputation and relative worth of a man of letters, the local and topical is inevitably separated out from that which is more universal, and more appealing to all ages and conditions of men. Were *Animal Farm* and *1984* the great successes which they were because of the immediacy of their appeal, as they were published just at the point where the full chaos and danger of the postwar world, with its confrontation between former allies of East and West, was becoming clear? Or do these books have a more timeless appeal? Just as Swift's *Gulliver's Travels* contains much local **satire** of English political and religious controversy of the early part of the eighteenth century, so Orwell's writing contains similar material. But what of its universality? This is the question which a critic must answer at some point when dealing with Orwell. Put another way, was Orwell a brilliant but ephemeral journalist, or did the body of his work have more solidity than is represented by even brilliant journalism which, after all by definition, appeals to the moment and not to the long view of history?

Orwell was written about during his lifetime, and John Atkins attempted to summarize some of the views expressed about him in his book, *George Orwell: A Literary and Biographical Study*, which is a rather ambitious work, and this may be consulted. Lionel Trilling, in his well-known essay, "George Orwell and the Politics of Truth," said with economy and restraint what many have said about Orwell: that he was an honest and honorable man as well as an honest man of letters. The entire point of the essay, which Professor Trilling originally wrote as an introduction to *Homage to Catalonia,* may be summed up in the words of one of his students about Orwell which Trilling himself quotes: "He was a virtuous man." For Professor Trilling, Orwell was not a genius. He was a committed man, in the sense that he lived his vision, as have Thoreau, Mark Twain, Walt Whitman, and perhaps Henry James, among major American writers of the past century. Orwell, in fact, was more modern than these; he was "engaged" in the sense that some of the Existentialists have been engaged and committed to political thought and action for the betterment of human life, whether or not they believed at the time that betterment was possible.

All of Orwell's writing, as Professor Trilling and others have indicated, was directly related to political ends which would have as their final result the promotion of human decency. To repeat a most important point: perhaps there is a lack of really enlightening critical writing about *Animal Farm, 1984* and other works of Orwell because he was so clear and precise as a writer. Valuing clearness, simplicity, and precision of expression over anything else in the technical craft of writing, Orwell may have said what he had to say in such a forceful way that interpretation was not as necessary as it might be in dealing with more complicated, allegorical, "literary" writers.

Sir Richard Rees was a close friend of George Orwell, and it has been said that he is one of the characters, Ravelston, in *Keep the Aspidistra Flying*, though this is not proven. It is significant that the title of Sir Richard's book is *George Orwell: Fugitive from the Camp of Victory*. For Orwell, the just man would not be found in the camp of victory, perhaps because in a state of perfect justice (the opposite of *1984*, and of Napoleon's regime in *Animal Farm*, which are both states of perfect injustice) there would be no camps of strong and weak, no exploiters and exploited, as occurs "naturally" in *Animal Farm* once the Revolution has come and gone. Thus, the interpretation of Orwell by Sir Richard Rees involves his view that Orwell was always self-motivated to stand up for the weak against the strong, though this has occasionally led to his actual political position being misinterpreted.

Special problems in the interpretation of *Animal Farm* have been dealt with in the appropriate sections of the present study.

But the critical axioms with which the reader should approach Orwell seem reducible to the following: Orwell's biography is very important, as he was above all a writer who lived his work. Second, Orwell's work is a "seamless garment" in which every part of it has a bearing on every other part, and all of his work leads up to his two masterpieces, *Animal Farm* (much the shorter, containing only some 30,000 words), and *1984,* for which he is best known. And third, Orwell's purpose in writing was not only to record what was happening in the world and to project ahead in order to make men realize what was happening and likely to happen; it was as much or more his purpose to change the world. He hoped that if he painted political evil vividly enough, men would turn from that evil. This is the ultimate justification for *Animal Farm,* though a story that will also double as a children's story has a double strength.

Animal Farm, as a political allegory, of course needs more historical interpretation than does *1984* in terms of the historical meanings of particular characters and events. These meanings have been given here, though of course this study does not pretend to have the final word on all of them. The difference between the two best-known and most powerful works of Orwell is that they are not only of a different **genre** - the beast - fable and the anti-Utopian fiction - but also *1984* seems to have more universal satirical meanings. Both books deal with what Orwell called "the central question - how to prevent power from being abused." This has been said before; it is quite important in understanding both. Further, both deal with the corruption of an originally revolutionary ideal into just another dictatorial regime, as though, Orwell is saying, men will always allow themselves to be tricked and to behave, in the terms of *Animal Farm,* like Boxer and the sheep. Orwell then had no easy answers to the overwhelming central question which he put concerning power and its abuses. But he could at least ask it in such a way that his contemporaries could see the absolute importance of the question, and this he did, in language too clear for conventional criticism.

As John Atkins pointed out in his work previously cited, he believes all of Orwell's work as a writer to have been preparation for the writing of his two masterpieces. The point which is quite important to the present discussion is that Atkins believes that the "book within a book," The Theory and Practice of Oligarchical Collectivism, allegedly written by Emmanuel Goldstein but almost certainly written by members of the Inner Party of *1984*, is the best key to the understanding of the structure and the political **satire** of *1984*. "Since the end of the Neolithic Age, there have been three kinds of people in the world, the High, the Middle, and the Low... ." This is the beginning of the first chapter of Goldstein's book.

Atkins accepted the thesis of Goldstein's book as one held by Orwell himself: that the end of power is power, that revolutions corrupt those who lead them, that the Low simply exchange one set of harsh masters for another in a revolution. These thoughts are at the center of *Animal Farm* as well, which ideologically if not in literary **genre** is closely related to *1984*. It is therefore suggested that *Animal Farm* and *1984* be read together, but probably *Animal Farm* should be read first. *1984* treats more elaborately the process of reality control, Doublethink, and the deception of the masses symbolized by Squealer in *Animal Farm*. Napoleon, of course, bears a striking resemblance in action if not in appearance to Big Brother. In short, the books form a unit; they demonstrate two perspectives, two ways of looking at the same thing, which in both cases is the modern totalitarian state.

A SELECTION OF VIEWS ON ANIMAL FARM

John Atkins

In his work George Orwell (see Bibliography below), Mr. Atkins includes an entire chapter on *Animal Farm*. He refers the reader, for historical aspects of the **satire**, to Louis Fischer's *The Life and Death of Stalin*, and to David J. Dallin's *The Real Soviet Russia*, and these are certainly among the good source books for a study of the history concerned. Atkins accepts the interpretation of the **satire** of *Animal Farm* as existing on a number of levels, one of which is of course the history of Stalinist Russia. It contains most of Orwell's major ideas about politics, according to this interpretation, which from all the evidence available certainly appears a correct one.

The hymns of praise dedicated to Napoleon have their parallels in history; Atkins, quoting a poem dedicated by the Russian poet Mayakovsky ("Minimus"?) to Stalin, makes this clear:

The world has no person Dearer, closer. With him, happiness is happier, And the sun brighter.

This may be compared with the ode composed by Minimus and dedicated to Napoleon, beginning: "Friend of fatherless! Fountain of happiness!" and entitled Comrade Napoleon, appearing in Chapter Eight of *Animal Farm.* But in general Atkins follows what is the main line of interpretation of *Animal Farm* in seeing in that book the levels of **satire** and the levels on which it may be comprehended, from the childhood fable to the serious, even profound, political commentary and commentary on human nature and the fate of revolutions.

Sir Richard Rees

In *George Orwell: Fugitive from the Camp of Victory*, Sir Richard makes a valuable contribution when he alludes to what Orwell himself said in a preface to the Ukrainian edition of *Animal Farm*. Orwell's view of the common man had undoubtedly become darker after the early 1940s, in part due to his deepening pessimism on the basis of his own experience. Boxer, a kindly, energetic, but essentially dim-witted horse works himself literally to death for his masters, believing that "Napoleon is always right." Orwell, in the Ukrainian edition, made reference to his experience in Spain, in which the P.O.U.M., including some of his friends, perished because they came into conflict with Stalinism whereas all they wanted was to get on with the fight against the common enemy of the Spanish Republic.

Rees interpreted the game of cards at the end of *Animal Farm* which led to the break-up of the banquet between humans and pigs as having an affinity with the Teheran conference. Rees, who was Orwell's personal friend, says that Orwell had the idea for *Animal Farm* when he served in Spain, and that he thought it over for six years before writing it-in the meantime, his opinions had changed somewhat in the direction of pessimism. Just as in *1984* when the Proles, ostensibly those for whom the Revolution was made, had fallen under the domination of a tyranny even worse than anything in the past, so in *Animal Farm* the ordinary residents of the Farm, once they have overthrown Jones, allow themselves to be hoodwinked and then enslaved by a gang of pigs. And Rees attributes this pessimistic conclusion to Orwell's own experiences, primarily in Spain, and to his reading of history in the light of such experience.

Christopher Hollis

In Chapter 12 of Mr. Hollis' study of George Orwell, we find some very useful personal reminiscences-Orwell was a schoolmate of Christopher Hollis at Eton, and while Hollis did not agree in many particulars with Orwell, especially on the subject of politics, the book is a useful one, then, as Chapter 12 applies specifically to *Animal Farm.*

Hollis sees great good fortune for both Orwell's purse and his reputation in the fact that the book was rejected by four publishers, and only published by Secker and Warburg in the exact month in which Germany surrendered, coinciding precisely with the beginning of popular disillusionment with Russia. One important interpretation, not alluded to before, relates *Animal Farm* to Orwell's interest in James Burnham's ideas as expressed in the book the *Managerial Revolution*, which Orwell himself had reviewed in a "little magazine' in 1946. Burnham's thesis was that the managers, after getting rid of the old proprietary exploiters, establish themselves in power as a new governing class-just as the pigs do in *Animal Farm.*

Hollis considers *Animal Farm* to be a great work of art rather than simply an ephemeral political tract. Orwell had said that *Animal Farm* had been a conscious fusion of political purpose and artistic purpose. Mr. Hollis shares the view held by others, including the writer of the present study, that in *Animal Farm* Orwell attained such perfection of technique within the limits of his political purpose that the book deserves to be called a classic, and will probably endure as such.

Further, Hollis believes *Animal Farm* to be a **satire** on all totalitarianism, and not simply communism; this squares with the most convincing reading of Orwell's life and works, and especially with a valid reading of *Animal Farm*.

Richard J. Voorhees

In *The Paradox of George Orwell*, Professor Voorhees gives it as his opinion that *Animal Farm*, because Orwell made it sound too convincing on the concrete level, has largely been relegated to the status of a children's work. Further, he thought Arthur Koestler's *Darkness at Noon* to be a more convincing critique of totalitarianism than *Animal Farm*. But little evidence is adduced to support this largely subjective contention. The beast-fable if it is written by a master arouses a willing suspension of disbelief. We know that pigs cannot walk on two legs and wield paintbrushes. This simply isn't the point. A psychological explanation for the effect which a good animal fable or tale has in conveying ideas is probably more useful than is an approach of the kind which Mr. Voorhees took in his study.

Probably the serious student of *Animal Farm* would be better advised, if he wishes not only to master the book but also to learn, or reinforce his knowledge of, the recent history of Russia, to read at least one of the studies of Russian history of the period from which Orwell took his material for *Animal Farm* listed in the Bibliography below. Especially recommended are the works by Louis Fischer.

ANIMAL FARM

Question: What is the evidence that *Animal Farm* was intended by Orwell as a political satire?

Answer: The most important evidence for this reading of *Animal Farm*, which may be said to be self-evident, lies in the biography of Orwell himself; in the totality of his life and his literary work other than *Animal Farm* itself. Almost everything Orwell ever wrote, including even critical essays ostensibly on purely literary subjects, such as his essay "Inside the Whale," had a political purpose. For Orwell, who was not typical, in this respect, of most Western writers of the twentieth century, literature and politics were closely related. Even an author who professed to have no political intention or **themes** was, for Orwell, by that very posture making a political judgment.

Orwell's summmum bonum, or "highest good' in his ethical system, seems to have been a state of society in which justice was one and in which there was no inequality or exploitation or oppression. Most Utopian writers, in fact all of them, by definition, have posited a societal structure of this kind, though the ways in which they thought it might be realized have been many and various. For some, Utopia would be a theocratic state; for others, such as Plato in his *Republic,* a form of society in which the rule would be exercised by philosopher-kings basing their decisions on an abstract Justice stemming from a kind of natural law. But Orwell was only distantly a Utopian writer; his two masterpieces are both in the nature of anti-Utopias: *Animal Farm* satirically and *1984* more elaborately and more directly. For Orwell thought that before Utopia could be brought about- if it could, given the nature of man - the modern drift toward totalitarianism must be reversed. And the only way it could be reversed, in his view, was by making men aware of the nature of totalitarianism and the destructive effects which came from it: oppression, power-worship, toadyism to a quasi-divine Leader, and terrorism, all of which Orwell took axiomatically as being evil in themselves.

Thus, as Orwell himself said in the essay "Why I Write," published after the completion of *Animal Farm,* every line which he had written since 1936 (that is, since the beginning of his participation in the Spanish Civil War and his acquaintance with totalitarianism firsthand), had been written, directly or indirectly, "against totalitarianism, and for democratic socialism." This is the ultimate justification for *Animal Farm's* satire; the reason behind it. It is entertainment, in a way, while *1984* with its deeper gloom cannot be so described. But basically *Animal Farm* is a serious political **satire** about the perversion of an originally idealistic Revolution which results in worsening the lot of the ordinary man rather than bettering it.

Question: Who are Pilkington of Foxwood and Frederick of Pinchfield?

Answer: These are farmers who are the closest neighbors of Mr. Jones and whose farms adjoin *Animal Farm.* It is clear from the thread of the historical **satire** that they represent respectively the Governments of Great Britain and of Germany at the time prior to and during the Second World War. The two are distinguished one from the other by the fact that Foxwood is larger and somewhat less efficiently run than Pinchfield, that Pilkington is a gentleman-farmer who spends much time hunting and fishing and rather less on strict business than does Frederick (whose name is probably meant to suggest Frederick the Great of Prussia, founder of the modern German state). Frederick spends much time on lawsuits, and is a quarrelsome man who drives a hard bargain. The animals dislike Pilkington as a human, but they are much more afraid of Frederick, on whose farm, they have heard, hideous tortures are practiced on the animals (Hitler's setting up of concentration camps, his persecution of national and religious groups which he disliked, etc.).

Napoleon, the boar and the Leader of Animal Farm, vacillates between Pilkington and Frederick, trying to play one against the other in a game of pure power politics, as Stalin did in the period prior to the Second World War. Napoleon concludes a business deal with Frederick, but is double-crossed by him and attacked without warning. This represents the Russo-German pact prior to the war, which was violated by Hitler on the basis of the Machiavellian dictum that it pays rulers to honor the treaties they have signed only as long as it pays them to do so, and not a moment longer. But the animals of Animal Farm fight heroically, especially Boxer, against Frederick. Ultimately Frederick is defeated, as was Hitler. Pilkington is received as an ally at a magnificent banquet by Napoleon (possibly the Teheran Conference). But there they quarrel bitterly as the book ends, for both of them want the same thing: world power and domination.

Question: Why is the setting of Orwell's **satire** a farm?

Answer: This question may seem to have a self-evident answer, but it has to do with a literary tradition of long antiquity. When an author wishes to construct a microcosm of society two "frame" devices stand ready to his purposes: the ship and the farm. One may think of Hawthorne's The Blithedale Romance, based on an actual Utopian experiment in plain living and high thinking at Brook Farm in the last century. Of course there is the frame device of the ship as well, from Sebastian Brant's Ship of Fools in the fifteenth century to Melville's Moby Dick in the last century and Joseph Conrad's novels, or many of them, in our own. In either case, whether the "frame" is a farm or a ship, the idea is simply to have a relatively small, and thus manageable and identifiable group, relating to each other in a way that more universal truths about human society and human relations are revealed. Both the farm and the ship are somewhat isolated from everyday society, a necessity for this kind of literary requirement.

Question: What is the relationship between *Animal Farm* and *1984*?

Answer: The two books are both Orwell's masterpieces, although he is probably better known for the latter. Both deal with "the central question: how to prevent power from being abused," to quote Orwell himself. Each of the books employs a different satiric method in pursuit of this end; *Animal Farm* is a beast-fable while *1984* is an anti-Utopia.

Animal Farm, unlike *1984*, may be read on the level of sheer entertainment; it would be possible for young children to read *Animal Farm* without any awareness of the political **satire**, just as *Gulliver's Travels* is often read on this level. *Animal Farm* is simpler in its statement of Orwell's political views, and as it was the earlier work in point of composition, should probably be read before *1984.*

There are many similarities between the two works. In both, there is an originally idealistic Revolution which has become corrupt; in both, there is an all-powerful Leader who has seized and maintained power by force, guile, and terrorism. The general population in both cases, for whom the Revolution was ostensibly made, is oppressed and terrorized so that any expressions of independent opinion may have the most dire consequences. Finally, in both Orwell shows the perversion of a noble idea: human equality and fraternity, into a sinister myth bearing no relation to the actual situation, and purveyed by a propaganda agency (the Ministry of Truth in *1984* and Squealer in *Animal Farm)* which has in each case the task of deceiving the general population. There are many other parallels as well as significant contrasts between the two masterpieces, but these are some of the more important.

Question: Whom do Snowball and Napoleon represent?

Answer: It is rather clear that the first represents Leon Trotsky and the second Josef Stalin. The history of the intrigues which led to Stalin's succession after Lenin as the ruler of the Soviet Union, and his maintenance in power for some three decades, is a fascinating one and may be studied in the books of Louis Fischer, David J. Dallin, Edmund Wilson (among those cited in the Bibliography of the present study) and many others. Leon Trotsky's own study of Stalin is valuable in this regard.

The evidence for the equation of Snowball with Trotsky and Napoleon with Stalin comes from a consideration of the personal characteristics which Orwell attributed to his animal characters. Like Trotsky, Snowball was a great organizer and led the revolutionary army during the early days of the Soviet regime, and was recognized as a hero who may have saved the regime, although later the official histories were rewritten to make him out as an archtraitor. Trotsky seems to have been more creative and more ready to formulate new plans than was Stalin, and this is carried over into the picture of Snowball. But Stalin, on the other hand, knew how to forge a Party apparatus and a system of Secret Police in order to attain power and force his rival out. This is exactly what Napoleon does in *Animal Farm.* He is ready to take over such ideas of Snowball as he can use-such as the windmill - but he arranges to receive the credit himself for these achievements, just as to Stalin were attributed all useful sciences and arts during the period of "the cult of personality" in the Soviet Union.

Question: What is the place of Squealer in *Animal Farm*?

Answer: Squealer represents any totalitarian Ministry of Propaganda, in Orwell's view; his analogue in *1984* is the Ministry of Truth. His function is to distort reality and to rewrite history in such a way that written documents (e.g. the Seven Commandments of Animalism) are constantly changed in order retroactively to bring them into conformity with Party policy. He is an important character in the microcosmic world of Animal Farm, perhaps second in importance to Napoleon himself.

The idea which Squealer represents - that there is no objective truth, and that the truth is what the Party says it is at the moment (subject to additional change and modification) - was a key one in Orwell's critique of totalitarianism. He found the negation of objective truth very disquieting - more so even than bombs or bullets - because it seemed to him that if a clever and unscrupulous totalitarian Leader and Party could gain power they could, using Squealer's methods of reality-control and reality-distortion, maintain themselves in power indefinitely. Orwell carries this idea much further in *1984*, but it should be recognized that this is quite important in the satire of *Animal Farm*.

Question: What is the function of the four human characters who have "speaking parts" in *Animal Farm*?

Answer: These are Farmer Jones, Lawyer Whymper, Pilkington of Foxwood, and Frederick of Pinchfield. All four are used as foils by Orwell; they serve as comparison and contrast with the animal characters. At the end, it is "impossible to say which was which" as between humans and animals. For the humans embody greed, incompetence, drunkenness, and treachery. The humans and the animals are presented as being motivated by the same unworthy drives and wishes. Orwell's satiric point seems to be that one may expect humans to live more according to reason and according to some moral standard than one expects, by definition, of animals, who are not "capable of reason" as are humans. But at least in the field of political affairs and especially of international relations, the law of the jungle prevails, there is no honor among thieves or between men and men or men and animals. Instead, there is mere anarchy based on self-interest, in Orwell's view. Men are no better than animals in this respect, yet they should be better if the long history of human civilization means anything.

Question: Relate Lord Acton's thesis to *Animal Farm*.

Answer: "Power corrupts, and absolute power corrupts absolutely," This aphorism was stated by Lord Acton in the last century, and seems to have been much on Orwell's mind as he wrote both *Animal Farm* and *1984*. In *Animal Farm,* there is initially, as in pre-1917 Russia, a relative power-vacuum, due to the unwillingness and inability of Farmer Jones to exercise the power which he must exercise by the requirements of his position. Power is seized spontaneously by the animals, out of idealistic motives and with the intention of following the rather lofty principles of Animalism which has been stated in Old Major's speech and in the "dream" which he had. But immediately the jockeying for power and position begins, until one of the characters, Snowball, is forced out and another, Napoleon, becomes supreme. Instead of exercising power in the name of all and on behalf of all, Napoleon uses his position to obtain more and more special privileges for his "class" and himself, using the agency of Squealer to justify this seizure.

So, Orwell implies, are all revolutions corrupted. He says that the only possible antidote to this rather depraved tendency, rooted perhaps in fundamental human nature (for Orwell seems to have believed in a secular sense in the Fall of Man), is something he repeatedly called "democratic socialism." But it is never clear, in any of Orwell's writings, what he meant by this. Essentially it may be that he was basically conservative, a position which he attributed to Charles Dickens in his essay on that writer: "If people would behave decently things would be different." This position really calls for a change of heart rather than a change of social system, and while Orwell seemed to attribute the corrupting effects of power both to human nature and to the social system, he was more successful in station the problem so graphically that his work will not soon be forgotten than he was in proposing any clear solution to the problem of the abuse of power which he saw as the very central question of our civilization.

Question: How may the character of Boxer be interpreted?

Answer: Orwell seems to signify by him the unthinking masses, in whom ultimate power resides if they would only become self-aware, but who are not likely ever to do so (see the treatment of the Proles in *1984)* as they are oppressed with drudgery and are not smart enough to see through the Napoleons of this world.

Boxer has the virtues Orwell attributed to the masses: simple loyalty ("Comrade Napoleon is always right,") and unselfish willingness to expend his strength in the service of his country which more sophisticated characters will sometimes refuse to do, according to Orwell ("I will work harder"). Yet Boxer does not know his own strength, allows himself to be shamefully, even cruelly exploited; and when his strength, used up in the service of *Animal Farm,* is gone he is cynically cast aside by Napoleon, who has been so corrupted by power that he has no sense of obligation to Boxer for all of the heroic work which he had done over the years. He is sold to the knacker, and the pigs use the money obtained from the sale to buy a case of whiskey and have another drunken party.

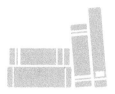

STUDY GUIDE

SELECTED BIBLIOGRAPHY

Works By George Orwell (Editions cited below should be easily available in the United States).

Orwell, George. *Nineteen Eighty-Four.* New York: Harcourt, Brace & World, Inc., 1949. Reprinted by Signet Books: The New American Library of World Literature, Inc., New York, N.Y., 1950.

____. *The Orwell Reader: Fiction, Essays, and Reportage.* Ed. by Richard H. Rovere. New York: Harcourt, Brace & World, Inc., Harvest Books, 1956.

____. *A Collection of Essays.* Garden City, N.Y.: Doubleday and Co., Doubleday Anchor Books, 1954. (Includes "Politics and the English Language" and "Such, Such Were the Joys …")

____. *The Road to Wigan Pier.* New York, N.Y.: Harcourt, Brace and Co., 1958. (First Published in England, 1937; see the Introduction by Victor Gollancz also printed in the 1958 American edition.)

____. *England, Your England and Other Essays*. London: Secker and Warburg, 1953.

____. *Homage to Catalonia*. Boston: Harcourt, Brace & World, Inc. Reprinted by Beacon Press, 1952. Intro. by Lionel Trilling.

____. *Burmese Days*. New York: Harcourt, Brace & World, Inc. 1934; reprinted in Popular Library, New York, 1958.

____. *Animal Farm*. New York: Harcourt, Brace & World, Inc. 1946. Reprinted in Signet Edition, New American Library, N.Y. 1956.

____. *Keep the Aspidistra Flying*. New York: Harcourt, Brace & World, Inc. 1956; reprinted in Popular Library, New York, 1957.

____. *A Clergyman's Daughter*. American Edition: New York: Harcourt, Brace and Co., Inc. 1935.

____. *Critical Essays*. London: Secker and Warburg, 1946. (See especially the essays entitled "Arthur Koestler" and "Wells, Hitler, and the World State.")

____. *Down and Out in Paris and London*, 1933. Harcourt, Brace & World, Inc. Reprinted by Avon Publications, New York, N.Y.

____. *Coming Up for Air*. 1939. New York: Harcourt, Brace & World, Inc. Reprinted 1950: Avon Publishing Co., Inc., New York.

____. "Second Thoughts on James Burnham". (Magazine article in *Polemic*, Vol. III; printed separately by Socialist Book Center, 158 Strand, London, July, 1946. A very important pamphlet for the study of the relation between Burnham's ideas and the **satire** of both *1984* and *Animal Farm*.)

Works Of Special Interest In The Criticism Of Orwell's Political Theory

Burnham, James. *The Managerial Revolution*. New York: John Day and Co., 1941. (A work of great influence on Orwell's preoccupation with totalitarian forms of government and the way in which ruling hierarchies seize and maintain power. See also Orwell's own review of this book.)

Burnham, James. *The Machiavellians*. 1943. Reprinted 1963: Chicago: Gateway Editions, Henry Regnery Co. (A series of essays by Burnham developing some of his ideas about power, as illustrated in such political and social theorists as Dante, Machiavelli, Mosca, Sorel, and Pareto. Pareto's theory of "the circulation of the elites" is significant in the light of Orwell's use of a similar idea in *1984:* the means by which the Inner Party can maintain itself in power; the same comment applies to *Animal Farm.*

Koestler, Arthur, *Darkness at Noon*. Reprinted 1958: New York, N.Y.: Signet Books, The New American Library. (Written 1938-40; published 1941. An account of the Moscow Purge Trials of the 1930s in fictionalized form, of special interest for comparison with *1984* and *Animal Farm* especially with respect to brainwashing and "reality control.")

Biographical And Critical Works (Selected)

Atkins, John. *George Orwell: A Literary and Biographical Study.* New York: Frederick Ungar Publishing Co., 1954. (Rather extensive study of Orwell, with an overview of all of Orwell's works. Worth consulting on *Animal Farm.)*

Brander, Laurence. *George Orwell*. New York: Longmans, Green and Co., 1954. (Along with Atkins above, a major study, the chief difficulty of which may be simply that it was written too soon after Orwell's death to be able to take a proper perspective. Therefore, like Atkins, not definitive.)

ANIMAL FARM

Connolly, Cyril. *Enemies of Promise*. London, 1938: revised and reset, 1949: Routledge and Kegan Paul, Ltd. (Contains anecdotes of Orwell at Eton as well as a general view of education at Eton and other great English public schools, by a contemporary and friend of Orwell. Valuable as an aid in the assessment of the effect which Orwell's education had in his development as a writer and in his ideas of social class.)

Highet, Gilbert. *A Clerk of Oxenford*. New York: Oxford Univ. Press, 1954. (Contains an essay on Orwell entitled "The Outsider" on a good introductory level.)

Hollis, Christopher. *A Study of George Orwell*. Chicago: Henry Regnery Co., 1954. (Valuable for its reminiscences of Orwell at Eton; Mr. Hollis was also roughly Orwell's contemporary at Eton and kept in touch with him in later life. Mr. Hollis, who has been a Conservative Member of Parliament as well as an author, is helpful in evaluating *1984, Animal Farm,* and other works of Orwell from a point of view rather different from that held by his subject.)

Hopkinson, Henry Thomas. *George Orwell*. Published for the British Council and the National Book League by Longmans, Green and Co., No. 39 in the series, *Writers and their Works,* London, 1961. (A pamphlet, introductory in nature and intended for the general reader, which contains a selective bibliography and a list of Orwell's works, including the titles of his individual essays.)

Howe, Irving, *Politics and the Novel*. New York: Horizon Press, 1957. (Studies of a number of authors whose fiction involves political judgments, including Malraux, Silone, Koestler and, as a concluding essay, "Orwell: History as Nightmare.")

Rees, Sir Richard. *George Orwell: Fugitive from the Camp of Victory*. Carbondale, Illinois: Southern Illinois University Press, 1961. (Sir Richard was a friend of Orwell, and is thought to be present in disguised fictional form in *Keep* the *Aspidistra Flying*. He assisted Orwell during his last illness, and knew a great deal about Orwell's life and mentality. The book advances the thesis that Orwell's life can in part be explained by a sense of guilt fostered in him by his childhood, and by his public-school education, and that he voluntarily submerged himself in poverty in order to expiate his sense of guilt as well as to acquire material for his writing.)

Russell, Bertrand. *Portraits from Memory*. New York: Simon and Schuster, 1956. (Contains a note and comment on *1984* and its validity as a representation of certain tendencies in the development or deterioration of society in the twentieth century. Most of this material is, of course, Lord Russell's opinion rather than an attempt at an interpretation of *1984*.)

Trilling, Lionel. "George Orwell and the Politics of Truth." Commentary, March, 1952; reprinted in *The Opposing Self*, New York: Viking Press, Compass Books, 1955. (Excellent introductory and evaluative essay, often referred to in the discussion of Orwell's life and work.)

Voorhees, Richard J. *The Paradox of George Orwell*. West Lafayette, Indiana: Purdue University Studies, *Humanistic Series*, 1961. (An introductory study, of more limited scope than those by Atkins, Brander, or Sir Richard Rees. The bibliography of magazine articles is useful.)

Suggested Introductory Works Concerning The History Which Orwell Satirized In Animal Farm.

Dallin, David J. *The Changing World of Soviet Russia*. New Haven: Yale University Press, 1956.

Dallin, David J. *From Purge to Coexistence*. Chicago: Henry Regnery Co., 1964. (Contains much valuable material on the Purges and the Moscow Trials of the 1930s.)

Fainsod, Merle. *How Russia is Ruled.* Revised Edition: Cambridge, Mass., Harvard University Press, 1963.

Fischer, Louis. *The Life and Death of Stalin.* 1st ed. New York: Harper and Co., 1953.

Fischer, Louis. *The Life of Lenin.* New York and London: Harper and Row, 1964 (Highly recommended as an introduction to the key figure of the Russian Revolution.)

Mendel, Arthur P. *Essential Works of Marxism.* New York: Bantam Books (SC 125) 1961. (Edited by Professor Mendel with useful introductory comments, this collection of essays includes many of the basic documents of Communism beginning with *The Communist Manifesto.*)

Stalin, Josef V. *Foundation of Leninism.* New York: International Publishers, 1932. (A good representative sample of Stalin's orientation to Marxist theories of government, power, the state, etc.

Trotsky, Leon. *Stalin: An Appraisal of the Man and his Influence.* translated and edited by C. Malamuth. New York: Grosset and Dunlap, The Universal Library, 1941.

Wilson, Edmund. *To the Finland Station: A Study in the Writing and Acting of History.* New York, 1940; reprinted 1953 by Doubleday Anchor Books. (Valuable introductory study of the evolution of Communist theory from Vico and Saint-Simon through Marx, Engels, Lenin, and Trotsky. Very well-written.)

Wolfe, Bertram D. *Three Who Made a Revolution: A Biographical History.* New York: The Dial Press, 1948. (Useful comparative studies of Lenin, Trotsky, and Stalin.)

SUGGESTED TOPICS FOR FURTHER RESEARCH

1. Orwell's critique of Communism in *Animal Farm.*

2. The use of the beast-fable as a satiric instrument in *Animal Farm,* to include the history of this genre.

3. Orwell's use of psychology in *Animal Farm* and in other works.

4. *Animal Farm, 1984,* and Orwell's presentation of brainwashing and thought control.

5. The relationship of *Animal Farm* to

   a. *1984*

   b. "Politics and the English Language"

   c. *The Road to Wigan Pier*

   d. *Coming Up for Air.*

   e. *Homage to Catalonia.*

   f. *Down and Out in Paris and London.*

6. Satirical techniques in *Animal Farm.*

7. The relation of Orwell's biography to his writing.

8. Is *Animal Farm* merely children's entertainment? What is the evidence in this matter? Will *Animal Farm* endure as a classic, or is it too topical and local?

9.   Snowball and Napoleon as satiric characters.

10. *Animal Farm* and the history of

   a. The Russian Revolution.

   b. Other modern revolutions or political upheavals, especially in Spain and Germany, with which Orwell was familiar.

11. What are the political theses which Orwell expressed in *Animal Farm*?

12. Construct, from a reading of *Animal Farm* and other works of Orwell, a statement of his own political and social philosophy.

13. Which is the greater masterpiece: *1984* or *Animal Farm*?

14. The essential Marxist theses and their evident refutation in *Animal Farm*.

Printed in the USA
CPSIA information can be obtained
at www.ICGtesting.com
LVHW010850290923
759457LV00018B/754